RACE AND INEQUALITY

CHATHAM HOUSE SERIES ON CHANGE IN AMERICAN POLITICS

edited by Aaron Wildavsky
University of California, Berkeley

RACE
AND
INEQUALITY
A Study in American Values

PAUL M. SNIDERMAN
Stanford University
and
Survey Research Center
University of California, Berkeley

with

MICHAEL GRAY HAGEN
University of California, Berkeley

CHATHAM HOUSE PUBLISHERS, INC.
Chatham, New Jersey

RACE AND INEQUALITY
A Study in American Values

CHATHAM HOUSE PUBLISHERS, INC.
Post Office Box One
Chatham, New Jersey 07928

PUBLISHER: Edward Artinian
COVER DESIGN: Yaron Fidler
ILLUSTRATIONS: Adrienne Shubert
COMPOSITION: Chatham Composer
PRINTING AND BINDING: Hamilton Printing Company

LIBRARY OF CONGRESS CATALOGING IN PUBLICATION DATA

Sniderman, Paul M.
    Race and inequality.

    (Chatham House series on change in American
politics)
    Bibliography: p.
    Includes index.
    1. United States—Race relations—Public opinion.
2. Afro-Americans—Civil rights—Public opinion.
3. Equality—United States—Public opinion.
4. Public opinion—United States.   5. National
characteristics, American.   I. Hagen, Michael Gray.
II. Title.   III. Series.
E185.615.S585   1985   305.8'00973   85-24247
ISBN 0-934540-24-1

Manufactured in the United States of America
10   9   8   7   6   5   4   3   2   1

To
Daniel Absher
John Hansen
Roberta Holzwarth
Carol Olney

CONTENTS

FIGURES

TABLES

PREFACE

The need for another book on the American ethos is not obvious — a quote from Tocqueville has surely excused enough. Yet the best-known studies of American values — Seymour Martin Lipset's or David Potter's, for example — have an indirect quality. In exploring the commitments of Americans, they take account of many kinds of evidence: records of personal travels, diaries, content analyses of children's stories, and industrial production figures. They attend to virtually everything except what ordinary Americans have to say about what they believe. This limitation is built into any genuinely historical study, for the public opinion survey is only two generations old.

Using these surveys, social scientists have added much to our understanding of the American ethos. But in contrast to studies such as Donald Devine's or Herbert McClosky's, the approach that we intend to take is a focused one in two senses. First, rather than canvass values generally, we study them in a specific context, that of racial inequality. Second, rather than look at values in isolation, we want to consider their connection to questions of public policy.

What Americans have to say about the problem of inequality — about why blacks have less than whites — is what we want to explore. This is, frankly, a book of exploration. It is based on interviews with Americans from all walks of life, who have expressed their thoughts about the meaning of racial inequality in America; about what has produced it and what should be done about it. Any one person's ideas are too complex to understand, to appreciate the full play of his or her individual experience and hopes and misunderstandings. Curiously, the ideas of a thousand people may be simpler to grasp; sheer numbers help one to see what is the general tendency, what the idiosyncratic exception. And we have the attitudes of several thousand Americans to examine for clues.

Clues to what? To some basic habits of mind of Americans, we believe. These are long-standing ideas that make up an important part of a distinctively American outlook on individual achievement, personal responsibility, failure, and inequality. And so it is without apology for the inevitable and real limits of our study that we present our sense of how, in a country dedicated to the principle of equality, people account for the fact of racial inequality.

The basic idea for this book we owe to Charles Y. Glock. In an effort to get a new grip on racial prejudice he introduced the concept of explanatory modes and developed a set of questions to operationalize it. Thanks to J. Merrill Shanks, these questions were subsequently included in a study of the 1972 presidential election by the Center for Political Studies at the University of Michigan. We therefore happily number ourselves among those able to undertake their studies of American public opinion and politics, thanks to the National Election Studies.

In addition, the senior author owes a special debt to the Survey Research Center at the University of California in Berkeley. It is no small thing that one's own university should assist one's work; it is extraordinary that another university, under no obligation to help, should do so, and for no better reason than to facilitate research. The Survey Research Center's director, Percy Tannenbaum, has put together the two ingredients that make a center for research: encouragement and colleagues. Among these are Christopher Achen, Henry Brady, Philip Tetlock, Aaron Wildavsky, and James Wiley. We thank them for criticizing our work without sinking our spirits; conversely, for refraining from criticism and raising our spirits, we thank Barbara and Raymond Wolfinger.

In addition, the State Data Program of the University of California, Berkeley, provided invaluable assistance. We are also indebted, for the design of the figures, to Guillermo Ruiz.

To colleagues at Stanford we owe much: Richard Brody, our partner in research, encouraged us from the start, and read drafts closely and sympathetically; John Chubb, James Kuklinski, and Terry Moe gave us the benefit of exacting yet encouraging readings; and Heinz Eulau, former department chairman, and Gerald Lieberman, vice provost for research, came to our rescue with emergency funds.

This work began in the classroom. It is more fun, it seems, to do social science than to read it. Thanks to four gifted undergraduates, the opportunity arose to put this belief to the test. And it is only one measure of gratitude that this book is dedicated to them.

Finally, there is the senior author's chief off-campus collaborator—Susie. He is not sure how this work was done with her help; he is quite sure that it would not have been done without her.

CHAPTER 1
INTRODUCTION

"The Republic . . . is of all the governments the one that depends most on every part of society. Look at this country! The Republic is everywhere, in the streets as in Congress."[1] So Francis Lieber, a German intellectual on a visit to America, exclaimed to Tocqueville. We, too, believe the Republic is in the streets: that government is not confined to public officials, that it extends to the public's opinion. And it is the public's opinion about racial equality that interests us. Do blacks have an equal chance to get ahead? What should be done to overcome discrimination? Above all, why are blacks less well off than whites? The answers given these questions make clearer not only whether white Americans are in favor of equality but what being in favor of it means. And understanding better popular conceptions of equality matters. For many of the deep differences over equality arise not from opposition to, but belief in, egalitarianism.

AMERICAN SUPPORT FOR RACIAL EQUALITY: 1940S-1970S

Since Tocqueville, it has been said that Americans are egalitarian. Perhaps it is worth observing, then, that only recently can they be said to have accepted the principle of racial equality.

The change in American beliefs about racial equality in recent decades amounts to a transformation. The extent of this change is apparent in figure 1.1 on page 4, which presents trends in support for three facets of racial equality: open housing, school integration, and equal job opportunities.

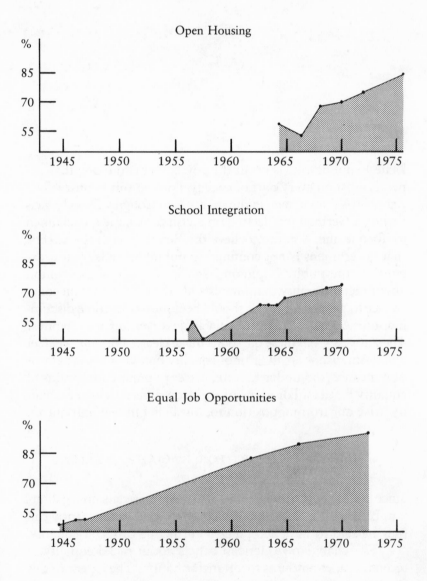

FIGURE 1.1
Trends in Support for Racial Equality

Consider the issue of open housing. Since 1964, at two-year intervals, the Center for Political Studies at the University of Michigan has asked representative samples of adult Americans which of these two statements they would agree with:

1. White people have a right to keep blacks out of their neighborhoods if they want to.
2. Blacks have a right to live wherever they can afford to, just like anybody else.[2]

The top panel in figure 1.1 charts changes in the percentage agreeing with the second of these statements from 1964 through 1976.[3]

In 1964 one American in four was opposed to open housing. A majority was in favor of it, to be sure, but it was neither solid—losing ground in 1966—nor overwhelming. After 1966, however, support for open housing mounted steadily. By 1976, less than one in ten Americans supported segregated housing, while an overwhelming number (85 percent to be exact) believed that blacks had the right to live wherever they could afford to, just like anybody else.

Data on American attitudes toward integration of schools and racial discrimination in employment show a similar trend. The middle panel of figure 1.1, drawing on the findings of a variety of major polling organizations from 1956 through 1970, reports the percentage of Americans who favor equality when asked, "Do you think white students and Negro students should go to the same schools or to separate schools?"[4] Again there is evidence of major change. In the mid-1950s, integration in the schools, even when considered in the abstract, free from the social pressures and personal costs of concrete choices, was supported by less than one-half of white Americans. By the end of the 1960s, it was approved by two-thirds or more of them.

The lower panel in figure 1.1 shows perhaps the most extraordinary of these changes in opinion, partly because it allows us to reach farther back in time. The figures record the percentage of white Americans favoring equality when asked, "Do you think Negroes should have as good a chance as white people to get any kind of job, or do you think white people should have the first chance at any kind of job?"[5] Note the alternatives: equal opportunity or preferential hiring for whites. In the mid-1940s, less than one-half of white Americans favored the principle of equal opportunity in employment; by the late 1960s (the next time the question was asked in a survey) over 80 percent supported it; and by the early 1970s, 95 percent backed it.

The sheer size of this change, however welcome to the proponent of equality, has had an ironic consequence: It makes it harder to discover where Americans stand on racial equality. Once it was sufficient to know whether their attitude toward the principle of racial equality was positive or negative. No longer; now that nearly all accept, or say they accept, the principle, it is necessary to know what they think it means. For obviously people can accept the principle of racial equality yet understand it to mean different things.

The stumbling block is focusing on equality as a value; white Americans have come to favor it, or have learned to say they do. Accordingly, we must ask, not whether Americans are in favor of racial equality but what they think being in favor of it means.

How to do this? Two strategies suggest themselves. One is to start with the fact of inequality and ask what should be done to overcome it. The focus, on this approach, is on equality as policy: What programs should be undertaken to realize equality, by whom, for whose benefit, and at whose expense? A second strategy shares the same starting point—acknowledging the fact of inequality. But rather than ask what should be done about inequality, this second approach asks instead: Why is there inequality? Why are blacks worse off than whites?[6]

Focusing on what should be done about racial inequality is a good way to talk to policy makers; this approach concentrates the mind on tradeoffs among values and opportunity costs and limited resources. But focusing on why blacks are worse off is a better way to talk to the average citizen. Without requiring an appreciation of niceties of policy analysis, it directs attention to what is, after all, fundamental: What does the fact of inequality, of real and stubborn racial inequality, in a society dedicated to the value of equality say about the character of that society?

Two Models of Public Opinion: Minimalist and Maximalist

Our concern is with how white Americans account for inequality, with how they explain why blacks have less than whites. But is it reasonable to think that the public at large has a real opinion, a coherent view, on the causes of inequality? The average citizen is hardly likely to have looked into them—indeed, is most unlikely to know more about them than he or she knows about most political questions. To determine whether the public is likely to have a genuine opinion about the reasons for racial inequality in particular, it is necessary to know the limits of public opinion in general.

One view of public opinion—the minimalist model, we shall call it—stresses how little the average citizen knows about politics and, accordingly, how his or her opinions about politics are often superficial, ephemeral, and minimally organized.

TABLE 1.1
Knowledge about Government

	Percentage Knowing the Right Answer
How many times can an individual be elected President?	74
Which party had the most members in the House of Representatives before the election?	64
Which party elected the most members to the House of Representatives in the election?	56
How long is the term of office for a member of the House of Representatives?	32
How long is the term of office for a U.S. Senator?	30

SOURCE: Reprinted by permission from Raymond E. Wolfinger, Martin Shapiro, and Fred I. Greenstein, *Dynamics of American Politics,* 2d ed. (Englewood Cliffs, N.J.: Prentice-Hall, 1980), 126. Copyright 1980 by Prentice-Hall, Inc.

The minimalist model rests on four sets of findings. The first concerns the lack of political knowledge. How much does the average American know about politics? Very little, it seems, even about elementary facts of political life. Table 1.1 on page 7 shows the number knowing the right answer to five simple questions about American politics.[7]

Citizens are not altogether ignorant; three-quarters know an American President can serve only two terms. But, then, only a third know that a representative's term is two years, a senator's six. It is not that these facts are vitally important to know. But the number of citizens who do not know them makes plain how little is known about even elementary and obvious facts of politics.[8]

To know whether the Democrats or the Republicans control the House of Representatives is not an unimportant piece of information. Without it, citizens may find it hard to know how to show approval, or express opposition, to national policy. In 1972, as table 1.1 shows, 56 percent knew which party had elected the most members to the House. This is not very many, considering that 50 percent, on average, would get the right answer by guessing.

Not only are many citizens ignorant about basic facts of American politics; they are ignorant of major issues as well. As table 1.2 shows, on average around one-fifth of the citizenry lack an opinion—that is, are unwilling to say whether they are pro or con—even on highly publicized political issues.

Obviously, there are issues on which practically everyone has an opinion; an example is busing. There does not, however, seem to be any relationship between the importance of an issue for the society and the number of citizens who are aware of it, even in the minimal sense of being willing to express an opinion about it.

Moreover, having an opinion about an issue is not the same as actually knowing something about it. *The American Voter* has estimated the number of citizens holding opinions on issues without having any idea as to what government was doing with respect to them.[9] The number of knowledgeable citizens varies, of course, with the specific issue. But on average, four in every

8

TABLE 1.2

Rates of Opinion Holding on Selected Issues

	Percentage with Opinions	Percentage without Opinions
Should women "have an equal role with men in running business, industry, and government?" (1976)	91	9
Do you favor "busing children to schools out of their own neighborhoods" to achieve racial integration?" (1976)	89	11
Should "the use of marijuana be made legal?" (1976)	86	14
Should the government "see to it that every person has a job and a good standard of living?" (1976)	80	20
Should there "be a government insurance plan which would cover all medical and hospital expenses?" (1976)	79	21
Should our farmers and businessmen "be allowed to do business with Communist countries?" (1968)	70	30
Is the government in Washington "getting too powerful for the good of the country?" (1976)	69	31
Should the U.S. "give aid to other countries if they need help?" (1968)	68	˙32
Where would you place yourself on a liberal to conservative scale? (1976)	67	33

SOURCE: Reprinted by permission from Robert S. Erikson, Norman R. Luttbeg, and Kent L. Tedin, *American Public Opinion,* 2d ed. (New York: Wiley, 1980), 22. Copyright 1980 by John Wiley & Sons, Inc.

ten citizens expressing an opinion about an issue are not knowledgeable about it. And counting those who express no opinion at all, that makes, on average, six in every ten citizens ignorant even of important and highly publicized issues.

9

A second line of research has documented the shallowness of public opinion. One indication is the extent to which answers to questions in opinion surveys can vary dramatically with changes in question wording or order. Studies have shown that even slight variations in questions can produce large variations in answers.[10] To mention one example among many, one study found that most Americans have a great deal of confidence in the armed forces if they are called the "army, navy, and air force," but markedly fewer do if they are called "the military."[11]

Another indication of shallowness is the instability of opinion on many issues. An extraordinary number of people do "change" their minds. In 1976, for example, the National Election Study asked a representative sample whether government should guarantee everyone a job and a good standard of living. Each person was asked the identical question twice: once shortly before the election, once shortly after it. As Erikson, Luttbeg, and Tedin report, only a third of those asked took the same side of the issue both times.[12]

The readiness of many people to take first one side of an issue, then the other, suggests that they may be making up their minds, so to speak, by flipping a coin, answering liberal if it comes up heads, conservative if it comes up tails. And when political positions are so lightly abandoned, Converse has argued, it would be prudent to recognize that for many they are, in reality, not positions at all.[13]

A third line of evidence supporting the minimalist position concerns the connectedness of political beliefs. Two kinds of connections are worth distinguishing. The first refers to connections among issue preferences. For example, will a person who favors an activist government to deal with the economy prefer an activist government to deal with education? The second refers to connections between issue preferences and general political orientations (e.g., partisanship or liberalism/conservatism). For example, will a person who sees himself (or herself), in general terms, as a liberal also take a liberal position on a specific issue, say, Medicare?

The first kind of connection has excited controversy, partly from the intrusion of methodological artifacts, partly from the absence of absolute standards of large and small. These points of uncertainty notwithstanding, the issue preferences of the public evidently are markedly less connected than those of political activists.[14]

The first kind of connection is the more controversial, the second the more important. A person who is unable to make the connections among issues lacks information; people who are unable to make connections between their general orientation and specific preferences lack direction. And there is good evidence that the average citizen often fails to make any connection whatever, between, say, the party he or she supports and the policies he or she favors.[15] Similarly, among the public at large, self-professed liberals not infrequently turn up on the conservative side of specific issues, with self-professed conservatives winding up on the liberal side.[16]

A fourth line of evidence favoring a minimalist position concerns understanding of abstract political ideas. As a practical matter, this comes down to an understanding of liberalism and conservatism. The basic finding, first reported by Campbell and his colleagues, is that only a fraction of Americans makes active use of categories like liberalism and conservatism in evaluating political parties or candidates.[17] And that fraction is, by any reasonable standard, not a large one; using the most generous criteria, only about one in every ten Americans makes any use whatever of any abstract evaluative categories (whether liberal/conservative or any other) in evaluating parties and candidates.[18] It is true that rather more are able to recognize these ideas and show, if prompted, that they have some sense of what they mean. But the important consideration, for our purposes, is not whether citizens are *able* to use master ideas like liberalism and conservatism to give order and coherence to their specific preferences; it is whether they *in fact* do so.[19]

A minimalist position, then, emphasizes four sets of findings: (1) the lack of political awareness among citizens at large; (2) the shallowness and instability of their political preferences; (3) the looseness of the connections among political ideas; and (4) their unfamiliarity with key political concepts, such as liberalism and conservatism.

A minimalist position paints an unflattering picture of citizens: ill-informed, superficial, inconsistent. This may, however, say more about the character of American politics than about the quality of citizens.[20] From this point of view, issues will not play an important role in citizens' views of politics if issues do not play an important role in politics. As Page and Brody were first to suggest, the American voter of the 1950s may have had cause not to see political parties or presidential candidates as offering clear-cut ideological choices; the purpose of campaigns was as much to obscure as to clarify where the candidates stood.[21] Nor was politics itself salient to the average citizen, given the general tranquility of the Eisenhower years. Things changed in the 1960s. The Johnson-Goldwater campaign, race riots and war protests, the insurgency campaigns of McCarthy and McGovern, Watergate, and a worsening economy—these were only some of the tumultuous events commanding public attention in the late 1960s and 1970s. They also reflected a politics that gave new prominence to the importance, and the connectedness, of issues. And consistent with a new politics of issues, Nie and his colleagues report a marked increase in the extent to which the beliefs of citizens were connected, beginning in 1964. Indeed, by their calculations, the attitudes of the public had become, by the late 1960s, at least as consistent as those of political elites had been in the late 1950s—and possibly even more so.[22]

Nie's thesis has a certain appeal, not least because it calls attention to the potential for variability in public opinion over time—a point, perhaps because of its obviousness, easily lost sight of. Intuitively plausible or not, Nie's thesis is not empirically compelling. Two groups of analysts have independently examined Nie's findings.[23] Both conclude that much of the apparent change in consistency between the 1950s and 1960s, far from reflecting a change in political consciousness, was simply occasioned by a change in question wording.

Much research on issue preferences, then, supports a minimalist model of public opinion; however, analysis of political attitudes favors a more maximalist one.[24] No one denies that citizens have attitudes in their heads that bear on politics—for example, racial prejudice, political cynicism, chauvinism and patriotism, political tolerance, orientations toward foreign policy such as isolationism and jingoism, and attitudes toward voting such as a sense of citizen duty and political efficacy. Certainly no one doubts that many citizens have genuine attitudes for or against abortion, legalizing marijuana, Medicare and welfare, tax cuts, busing, pollution, inflation and high prices, prayer in public schools—in a word, about a host of controversial issues in politics. The question at issue is the extent to which people see that these various attitudes are themselves connected, or "constrained," and make up "packages" of beliefs.

There are packages of belief, certainly in the area of politics of interest to us here: race. As Carmines and Stimson point out, not only was public opinion on racial issues highly constrained in the mid-1960s and early 1970s but it was highly constrained in the 1950s as well.[25] And Sears and his colleagues have uncovered a still larger package of beliefs: "symbolic racism," as they call it. This package is a mixture of racial and nonracial beliefs—in particular, of hostility to blacks and of support for conservative values—fused together in a belief that blacks are not willing to live by the basic values of this country and make it on their own. Moreover, symbolic racism, again according to Sears and his colleagues, is connected with voter preferences not only on racial issues like busing but also on ostensibly nonracial ones like tax cuts.[26]

Apart from the racial issue, are there packages of explicitly political beliefs of any appreciable generality and distinctness that ordinary citizens are likely to hold? The evidence on this question is rather thin as there have been few systematic, sophisticated studies of political values.[27] Nonetheless, at least one such package of beliefs shows up in the opinions of ordinary citizens. That package is "classical conservatism."[28]

Classical conservatism is only one dimension of liberalism/conservatism. Nonetheless, it constitutes a definite and familiar point of view in politics. The person conservative in this sense feels that the best guide to the future is past experience, not "abstract theory," as he or she would label it; that people are not really equal, and so some should play a larger part, others a smaller and subordinate one, in politics as in life generally; that preserving order and respecting authority are primary duties, and should be firmly enforced; that intellectuals are less dependable than the person with a practical mind and a proven track record; and that so-called reforms, instead of improving things, often make them worse and that it is therefore wise not to change unless it is absolutely necessary to change.

Classical conservatism is one element of the belief systems of many Americans. So, for that matter, are other aspects of liberalism/conservatism, including New Deal liberalism and the so-called social issues.[29] These various aspects of liberalism/conservatism seem to be imperfectly connected, though research on this is still too fragmented and forced to rely on measures too narrow to be considered conclusive. Even so, each of these aspects or elements of liberalism/conservatism is an example of a coherent package of beliefs, appearing with some definiteness and frequency in the belief systems of the public.

In addition to packages of beliefs, there is evidence of a second order of organization, of "packages of packages." Herbert McClosky and his colleagues have shown that one can identify and reliably measure, in general population surveys, coherent and broad-gauged orientations toward master ideas of politics such as democracy and capitalism.[30] The striking characteristic of such orientations, from our point of view certainly, is the amount of cognitive territory they cover; each takes in an extended range of ideas, preferences, values.

So McClosky's Democratic Values Scale reflects people's tendency to take a consistent and encompassing position on, among other things, the right of the media to employ radicals; the range of ideas to which children may properly be exposed; the use of federal agents to spy on radical organizations; the use of town halls by groups like the American Nazi party; provision of lawyers for all accused of a crime, at public expense if necessary; prayer in the public schools; obscenity and censorship; equal rights for homosexuals; police searches of homes or cars without a warrant; racially restrictive covenants; and the *Miranda* rule. A considerable assortment of issues by any standard. Nor are their connections all on the surface, obvious. Tying them together suggests organization of political thought.

McClosky's Capitalist Values Scale indicates a similar connectedness of political ideas in the minds of ordinary citizens. For it demonstrates a readiness on their part to form systematic, consistent ideas about a range of questions, including workers' rights in industrial decision making; the human (or dehumanizing) effects of the profit system; the power of trade unions; customary reasons for repeated failure; the importance of property rights to society as a whole; the equity of income inequality; the value of competition in school, work, or business; the legitimacy of strikes; and the fairness of taxes. Being able to pull together ideas about these questions, to appreciate what one has to do with another, is surely what we mean by connectedness.

Both packages of packages—orientations toward democracy and toward capitalism—are found among citizens at large, not just among political elites. This is not to say that these packages are as tightly tied together for the one as for the other. McClosky and his colleagues take pains to make plain that the connections among idea elements are weaker for ordinary citizens than for political activists; and not trivially but appreciably weaker.[31]

But if the connections among ideas are weaker, the pattern of association of ideas is similar. Less complete and intricate, in the case of the ordinary citizen, but similar all the same. So the person who favors a right to unlimited profit tends also to favor unrestricted competition *and* to emphasize the importance of hard work and self-reliance *and* to oppose government regulation *and* to defend unequal economic rewards, and so on. Many of the same ideas go together, in the same way (though not to the same degree) for the average citizen as for the political sophisticate.

The similarity of patterning between public and political elites suggests that there is some appreciable organization to the political ideas of ordinary citizens, for these ideas are put together in ways that are coherent by the standards of the politically sophisticated themselves.

IDEAS ABOUT RACIAL EQUALITY:
A MAXIMALIST POSITION

Which model of public opinion, then, is closer to the truth—
the minimalist or maximalist? This is, we suggest, the wrong
way to put the question. It is a mistake to ask if the one position is right, the other wrong. To choose between them is to
make a false choice. It does make sense, however, to ask: Under
what conditions is a minimalist model useful, and under what
conditions is a maximalist one appropriate?

The average citizen knows little about politics. Nor does
he or she pay much attention to it, even when something of
unusual interest is going on, like a presidential campaign. It
is only prudent, therefore, to take a minimalist position as one's
baseline expectation, one's best guess as to what public opinion is ordinarily like.[32]

There are, however, at least two conditions under which
a maximalist model is appropriate—and American ideas about
racial equality meet both.

The first condition is this: when issues explicitly involve
salient groups about which the public at large has strong feelings. The average citizen, though he (or she) may know little
about politics, knows whom he likes and, still more important perhaps, whom he dislikes. This can be a sufficient basis
for figuring out a consistent policy stance. The paradigmatic
example is racial attitudes, as Converse has pointed out.[33] The
person deeply committed to racially segregated housing is also
likely to be committed to racially segregated schools. In this
case, knowledge of the particulars of policy is not necessary
for citizens to develop a consistent position; they need to know
only whether a policy promises to increase the freedom of blacks
to live and work where they want to, plus, of course, whether
or not they dislike blacks. And it is precisely attitudes of this
sort that are central to American ideas about racial equality.
Not only do most know how they feel about blacks; they also
know how they feel about whether blacks have been unfairly
treated and what, if anything, should be done to see that they
are treated fairly now.

16

One consideration, then, is attitudes toward *whom;* another is attitudes toward *what.*

Strong evidence of minimal connectedness in the belief systems of the public is based on analysis of narrow political issues — federal housing policy, for example. Unconnected, however, hardly seems the way to characterize Americans' ideas about what is fair. Rather the reverse.[34] These ideas are so familiar, so much a part of what many are taught is right and proper, as to represent a folk ideology. This folk ideology includes, for example, ideas about whether the most important factor in getting ahead in life is luck, hard work, or family background; about whether the child of a factory worker has the same chance to get ahead as a child whose parents are well-off; about whether everyone should make the same amount of money or as much (and as little) as he or she can get paid; about when one should take care of one's own problems and when the government should help; and about whether people should try to overcome obstacles like discrimination on their own or join with others to fight them together.[35]

Citizens may not know much about politics; the popular culture is another story. The average citizen can make sense of the question "Why do some people have less than others?" not because he or she has been schooled in abstract theories of equality but because he or she has absorbed something of this culture. For it deals directly with ideas about success and failure — about the importance of individual effort, for example, as expressed in the conviction that anyone with talent and a willingness to work can get ahead in America. It is not necessary to go to college to hear about Horatio Alger.

The figure of Horatio Alger, of the self-made man, is a form of symbolic shorthand, a way of referring to a constellation of ideas about achievement. This constellation is a familiar one. It includes ideas emphasizing the importance of individual initiative, effort, and merit; of standing on one's own two feet and of persevering until one succeeds; of accepting responsibility for one's own fate and making the best of one's lot. These ideas give many Americans a tool for understanding why some succeed and others do not. And by virtue of their familiarity, no special insight into politics is necessary to learn them. Rather the contrary. These ideas are a staple of the popular culture and so are, if anything, more likely to be absorbed by those who are not highly educated or uncommonly involved in politics.

In sum: Citizens generally have minimal knowledge of political detail and minimally organized ideas on many issues of policy; nonetheless, they are likely to hold settled and coherent ideas as to why blacks are less well off than whites, for two reasons at least. First, the focus is on a specific and salient social group — blacks; second, the subject — reasons for achievement — is a prominent part of the popular culture.

THE DATA

The bases for our impressions of American ideas about inequality are two scientific surveys of public opinion. One is a national study, conducted by the Center for Political Studies at the University of Michigan;[36] the other is a regional study of the San Francisco-Oakland Bay Area, conducted by the Survey Research Center at the University of California at Berkeley.[37]

Let us say a word about these two surveys. Each is a cross-sectional sample of adult Americans, selected at random so as to be representative, in the one case of the country as a whole, in the other of the San Francisco-Oakland Bay Area. From first step to last — from design of the sample, questionnaire construction, pretesting, interviewer selection and training, to recording and "cleaning" of the data — both studies were carried out by university specialists in survey research to meet academic standards. In a word, the data are of uncommon quality.[38]

Both studies also were ambitious, which is, unfortunately, another way of saying they are complicated. The National Election Study, for the first and only time, asked certain questions of one-half the sample and other questions of the other half. This was done to increase, beyond those routinely pursued, the number of areas of belief that could be explored in an interview. The decision regarding who was to be asked what was made on a random basis, and so each half of the sample is itself a representative sample — but, of course, of only one-half the customary size. This limits the depth of analysis, but in no way weakens the main conclusions we report.

The Bay Area Study served as a platform for three separate studies: of prejudice, political alienation, and the status of women. In an interview of only one hour, divided into these three parts plus a fourth for background information, a few questions may be asked about many things — but not many questions about any one thing. The Bay Area Study, therefore, serves a secondary role: to confirm findings from the national study. Insofar as the results of the two correspond, we shall have more confidence that we really have got things right.

These two studies — the NES and the BAS — are, from one angle, investigations of two different worlds. Politically, the San Francisco Bay Area is more liberal than the country as a whole. It is also more activist: 20 percent of the adults in the Bay Area said they had participated in at least one kind of political protest in the 1960s, compared to less than 1 percent of adults in the country as a whole.[39] And the Bay Area participants are better educated. Again in 1972, 58 percent of the adults in the Bay Area said they had at least some college education, compared to 29 percent in the country as a whole. In the face of these (and other) differences, to observe that the tack people take in trying to explain racial inequality signifies much the same thing in the one survey as in the other would be an impressive finding indeed.

Public attitudes change with time, but our interest here is with American habits of mind, with long-standing convictions about individual achievement, personal responsibility, failure, and inequality. For this reason, the coincidence of two surveys being conducted at the same point in time, each entirely independent of the other, one of the country as a whole and the other of a part that seems idiosyncratic, is serendipity. For if the results of both studies are the same, our study will have a uniquely strong foundation.

Finally, a word about whose views on equality we are reporting: those of white Americans. The explanations blacks offer for racial inequality differ vastly from those that whites

19

give. And, unfortunately, there are too few blacks in the National Election Study sample, our primary source of data, for systematic analysis in their own right.[40]

THE ARGUMENT

To explore ideas about inequality is to study both political culture and public policy. What does such an undertaking involve? Neither institutional analysis of decision making nor psychological analysis of attitude formation, we suggest. The first is clear: Here we investigate not how specific laws are made or enforced but what the average citizen thinks about racial inequality, including the role (if any) of government in overcoming it. The second is less clear. It is well, therefore, to make plain what we are attempting and what we are arguing.

Americans, it turns out, find a variety of explanations for racial inequality credible. These range from God's will to economic exploitation. By looking at these explanations of inequality, we hope to be able to understand something of the nature of two of the principal elements of the American ethos: moralism and individualism.

There is certainly nothing novel in remarking the importance of the two; both individualism and moralism have been featured as distinctively American, and perhaps politically decisive, attitudes of mind.[41] But each of them has been studied in its own right, in isolation from the other.[42] Yet it is the interplay of ideas of responsibility and wrongdoing that opens to view points of affinity and antagonism between competing conceptions of individual need, desert, and potential. And it is this interplay of views, rather than any one view in itself, that has helped give American politics a special temper.

Our starting point is to explore a number of specific explanations for racial inequality. These include the legacy of past discrimination and slavery, God's will, exploitation, individual effort and persistence (or the lack thereof), differences in socialization, and inherent racial differences in ability. We want, first, to compare the popularity of these various explanations. Do more Americans believe that blacks are worse off than whites because of, say, economic exploitation or because of divine command? With these facts in hand, we can take the next step, and consider how these specific explanations may fit together.

Our working premise is this: Questions of responsibility and of wrongdoing go to the heart of efforts to account for the fact of racial inequality. How may the idea of responsibility be understood in this context? Certain staples of the American ethos set the terms of the debate for many. One is the ethic of self-reliance; another, the presumption of divine mandate for racial inequality. And to capture these long-standing, or traditional, habits of mind, we try especially to catch hold of two ways of explaining inequality: individualism and fundamentalism. In addition, there seem to us to be two other orientations toward inequality that have become prominent in arguments over the American dilemma. One of them—the historicist—sees present inequalities as archaic legacies of past discrimination. The other—the progressive—attributes the inequality of blacks to the workings of American society itself, and in particular, to economic exploitation.

Individualist and fundamentalist orientations draw on traditional themes in the American culture. In contrast, progressive and historicist are more modernist in spirit. Alongside this cleavage is another: between moralistic and nonmoralistic.

Moralism is a style of thought: a propensity to convert wrongs into wrongdoing, to explain why things are the way they are—and not the way they should be—by blaming somebody, not for being mistaken, but for being morally deficient. The problem of racial inequality, precisely because it is a moral issue, invites moralistic responses. In saying a response is moralistic we do not mean to suggest that it is for this reason in error or inappropriate. Rather, moralism is a useful category because it calls attention to a signal quality of the American political culture: its basis in Protestantism.

Students of American history and literature have long recognized the importance of religious forms in American politics.[43] Moralism sometimes assumes explicitly religious garb. But it presents itself in a secular as well as a religious form, allowing it to appeal to the political left as well as the right.

RACE AND INEQUALITY

Moralism is a curiously convoluted, even contradictory, style of political thought; indeed, it is contradictory on at least two levels. First, it is a style of thought appealing to a fundamentalist outlook on the one side, to a modernist on the other. And this first contradiction is the product of a second, deeper one. Moralism may be a hallmark of the American ethos, as many have observed, but one of its telltale qualities is precisely an antipathy to that ethos.

Antipathy to American society is not surprising in a person who believes that it is racially exploitative; however, it seems odd, even inconsistent, in a person who is a booster of traditional American values, among them religious and conventional moral values. But this inconsistency, we suggest, only points up the paradoxical nature of conventionality as a social attitude; for the person who insists on others' adhering to conventional American values is himself or herself unlikely to adhere to them.

Moralism is one of our main interests; individualism is the other. The idea that anyone can get to the top, provided only that he or she is willing to work, may not be an exclusively American idea. Yet it is so pervasive, so deep-lying, as to be a distinctively American one.

Individualism, we argue, undercuts efforts to realize racial equality not out of hostility to the idea of equality but for just the opposite reason: Individualism is itself a species of egalitarianism. Of course, some opposition to realizing racial equality springs from racial bigotry or from callousness and lack of empathy for the disadvantaged or from a failure to appreciate and to think through what the value of equality—and, for that matter, liberty—entails. But, we want to suggest, even were this a world free of prejudice and meanness of spirit and ignorance, there would still be opposition to realizing racial equality—an opposition rooted in egalitarianism in the form of individualism.

To see why this is so it is necessary to step back, to see how white Americans explain why blacks have less.

NOTES

1. George Wilson Pierson, *Tocqueville in America* (Gloucester, Mass.: Peter Smith, 1969), 248.
2. A third alternative was to answer "don't know."
3. The source of these data is Warren E. Miller, Arthur H. Miller, and Edward J. Schneider, *American National Election Studies Data Sourcebook* (Cambridge, Mass.: Harvard University Press, 1980), 177.
4. For compiling and reporting these data in his extremely useful and provocative article on this issue, we are indebted to Paul Burstein, "Public Opinion, Demonstrations, and the Passage of Antidiscrimination Legislation," *Public Opinion Quarterly* 43 (1979): 160.
5. Ibid., 163.
6. Charles Glock was the originator of this approach, as we noted in the preface. For a presentation of his independent studies, explicitly focused on the concept of explanatory modes, see Richard A. Apostle, Charles Y. Glock, Thomas Piazza, and Marijean Suelzle, *The Anatomy of Racial Attitudes* (Berkeley: University of California Press, 1983).
7. The findings, though typical, are of particular interest because they are based on the same national sample we used in our analysis.
8. Robert E. Lane and David O. Sears, *Public Opinion* (Englewood Cliffs, N.J.: Prentice-Hall, 1964).
9. Angus Campbell, Philip E. Converse, Warren E. Miller, and Donald E. Stokes, *The American Voter* (New York: Wiley, 1960).
10. For an up-to-date review of wording effects, see Howard Schuman and Stanley Presser, *Questions and Answers in Attitude Surveys* (New York: Academic Press, 1981).
11. Seymour Martin Lipset, "The Wavering Polls," in *Public Opinion and Public Policy,* ed. Norman R. Luttbeg (Itasca, Ill.: Peacock, 1981), 353-67.
12. Robert S. Erikson, Norman R. Luttbeg, and Kent L. Tedin, *American Public Opinion,* 2d ed. (New York: Wiley, 1980), 23.
13. See Philip E. Converse, "The Nature of Belief Systems in Mass Publics," in *Ideology and Discontent,* ed. David E. Apter (New York: Free Press, 1964). This is the celebrated nonattitude hypothesis. Not surprisingly, it has been challenged. An especially compelling and artful countercase is offered by Achen, who shows that the problem may reflect the flaws in the questions being asked rather than in the answers being given. See Christopher H. Achen, "Mass Attitudes and the Survey Response," *American Political Science Review* 69 (1975): 1218-31.
14. Converse, "The Nature of Belief Systems in Mass Publics"; Norman H. Nie and Kristi Andersen, "Mass Belief Systems Revisited: Political Change and Attitude Structure," *Journal of Politics* 36 (1974): 540-90; Norman H. Nie, Sidney Verba, and John R. Petrocik, *The Changing American Voter* (Cambridge, Mass.: Harvard University Press, 1976); John L. Sullivan, James E. Piereson, and George E. Marcus, "Ideological

Constraint in the Mass Public: A Methodological Critique and Some New Findings," *American Journal of Political Science* 22 (1978): 233-49; George F. Bishop, Alfred J. Tuchfarber, and Robert W. Oldendick, "Change in the Structure of American Political Attitudes: The Nagging Question of Question Wording," *American Journal of Political Science* 22 (1978): 250-69; John L. Sullivan, James E. Piereson, George E. Marcus, and Stanley Feldman, "The More Things Change, The More They Stay the Same: The Stability of Mass Belief Systems," *American Journal of Political Science* 23 (1979): 176-86; and George F. Bishop, Alfred J. Tuchfarber, Robert W. Oldendick, and Stephen E. Bennett, "Questions about Question Wording," *American Journal of Political Science* 23 (1979): 187-92.

15. Herbert McClosky, Paul J. Hoffman, and Rosemary O'Hara, "Issue Conflict and Consensus among Party Leaders and Followers," *American Political Science Review* 54 (1960): 406-27; and Converse, "The Nature of Belief Systems in Mass Publics."

16. Warren E. Miller and Teresa E. Levitin, *Leadership and Change: The New Politics and the American Electorate* (Cambridge, Mass.: Winthrop, 1976); McClosky et al., "Issue Conflict and Consensus among Party Leaders and Followers."

17. Campbell et al., *The American Voter*.

18. Ibid., 249; John C. Pierce and Paul R. Hagner, "Conceptualization and Party Identification: 1956-1976," *American Journal of Political Science* 26 (1982): 377-87.

19. Some, of course, do. But the best evidence suggests that most do not. In fairness, a number of studies of levels of conceptualization have argued that more citizens made use of master constructs like liberalism/conservatism in the 1960s and 1970s than earlier. John O. Field and Ronald E. Anderson, "Ideology in the Public's Conception of the 1964 Election," *Public Opinion Quarterly* 33 (1969): 380-98; and Nie et al., *The Changing American Voter*. Whether this actually happened is up in the air—where it is likely to remain; many of the measures of conceptualization have, unfortunately, been shown to be so unreliable as to be untrustworthy. Eric R.A.N. Smith, "The Levels of Conceptualization: False Measures of Ideological Sophistication," *American Political Science Review* 74 (1980): 685-96.

20. For example, see W. Lance Bennett, *Public Opinion in American Politics* (New York: Harcourt Brace Jovanovich, 1980).

21. Benjamin I. Page and Richard A. Brody, "Policy Voting and the Electoral Process: The Vietnam War Issue," *American Political Science Review* 66 (1972): 979-95; also see Benjamin I. Page, *Choices and Echoes in Presidential Elections* (Chicago: University of Chicago Press, 1978).

22. See Nie et al., *The Changing American Voter*, 136.

23. Sullivan et al., "Ideological Constraint in the Mass Public"; Bishop et al., "Change in the Structure of American Political Attitudes"; Sullivan et

al., "The Stability of Mass Belief Systems"; Bishop et al., "Questions about Question Wording."

24. Perhaps the best-known, certainly the most thoughtful, case for a maximalist position has been set out by Robert Lane. See, for example, Robert E. Lane, "Patterns of Political Belief," in *Handbook of Political Psychology*, ed. Jeanne N. Knutson (San Francisco: Jossey-Bass, 1973), 83-116. We shall confine ourselves to observing the findings of survey research, however, for there is general consensus that the case study tends to a maximalist model, but little awareness that quantitative designs have done so too.

25. Edward G. Carmines and James A. Stimson, "Racial Issues and the Structure of Mass Belief Systems," *Journal of Politics* 44 (1982): 2-20.

26. See, for example, John B. McConahay, "Self-Interest versus Racial Attitudes as Correlates of Anti-Busing Attitudes in Louisville: Is It the Buses or the Blacks?" *Journal of Politics* 44 (1982): 692-720; and David O. Sears and Jack Citrin, *Tax Revolt* (Cambridge, Mass.: Harvard University Press, 1982).

27. But see Ronald Inglehart, *The Silent Revolution* (Princeton: Princeton University Press, 1977); Milton Rokeach, *Belief, Attitudes and Values* (San Francisco: Jossey-Bass, 1968); and Milton Rokeach, *The Nature of Human Values* (New York: Free Press, 1973).

28. Herbert McClosky, "Conservatism and Personality," *American Political Science Review* 52 (1958): 27-45; and Herbert McClosky and Charles A. Bann, "On the Reappraisal of the Classical Conservatism Scale," *Political Methodology* 6 (1979): 149-72.

29. James A. Stimson, "Belief Systems: Constraint, Complexity, and the 1972 Election," *American Journal of Political Science* 19 (1975): 383-418.

30. Dennis Chong, Herbert McClosky, and John Zaller, "Patterns of Support for Democratic and Capitalist Values in the United States," *British Journal of Political Science* 13 (1983): 401-40; see also Herbert McClosky and John Zaller, *The American Ethos: Public Attitudes toward Capitalism and Democracy* (Cambridge, Mass: Harvard University Press, 1984); and Herbert McClosky and Alida Brill, *Dimensions of Tolerance* (New York: Russell Sage Foundation, 1983).

31. See especially, Chong et al., "Patterns of Support for Democratic and Capitalist Values."

32. Minimalist models and rational interpretations are not incompatible. See Morris P. Fiorina, *Retrospective Voting in American National Elections* (New Haven: Yale University Press, 1981); and Richard A. Brody and Paul M. Sniderman, "From Life Space to Polling Place: The Relevance of Personal Concerns for Voting Behavior," *British Journal of Political Science* 7 (1977): 337-60.

33. Converse, "The Nature of Belief Systems in Mass Publics."

34. Jennifer Hochschild, *What's Fair?* (Cambridge, Mass.: Harvard University Press, 1981).

35. Schlozman and Verba use the expression "social ideology." See Kay Lehman Schlozman and Sidney Verba, *Injury to Insult* (Cambridge, Mass.: Harvard University Press, 1979). Folk ideology, we think, better conveys the popular character of these ideas. See Stanley Feldman, "Economic Self-Interest and Political Behavior," *American Journal of Political Science* 26 (1982): 446-66; and Paul M. Sniderman and Richard A. Brody, "Coping: The Ethic of Self-Reliance," *American Journal of Political Science* 21 (1977): 501-21.

36. The National Election Study data were made available by the Inter-University Consortium for Political and Social Research. The Center for Political Studies of the Institute for Social Research at the University of Michigan collected the data for the 1972 American National Election Study under a grant from the National Science Foundation. We, of course, bear sole responsibility for the analysis here.

37. The Bay Area Survey data were made available by the Survey Research Center of the University of California at Berkeley. They too were collected under a grant from the National Science Foundation.

38. See appendix A for an overview of sampling design and data collection procedures.

39. For these figures, see Paul M. Sniderman, *A Question of Loyalty* (Berkeley: University of California Press, 1981).

40. Ten percent of the NES sample is black. In absolute numbers this means 267 people; and of course one-half of these were not asked the relevant questions.

41. A recent and especially ambitious interpretation of the dynamics of American politics, stressing moralism as an incendiary force, is offered by Samuel P. Huntington, *American Politics: The Promise of Disharmony* (Cambridge, Mass.: Belknap Press, 1981); a classic and uncommonly comprehensive survey of individualism in American history and literature is presented by Yehoshua Arieli, *Individualism and Nationalism in American Ideology* (Baltimore: Penguin Books, 1964).

42. Particularly impressive examples of this approach are Schlozman and Verba, *Injury to Insult;* and Stanley Feldman, "Economic Individualism and Mass Belief Systems" (paper prepared for delivery at the Annual Meeting of the Midwest Political Science Association, Cincinnati, Ohio, 15-18 April 1981). Each makes evident how much can be learned even in considering a major idea element (individualism, in this case) by itself.

43. Many works could be cited under this head. Here we mention only two scholars whose writing has had a special impact on us: Sacvan Bercovitch, *The American Jeremiad* (Madison: University of Wisconsin Press, 1978); and Perry Miller, *Errand into the Wilderness* (Cambridge, Mass.: Harvard University Press, 1956).

CHAPTER 2

EXPLANATIONS FOR RACIAL INEQUALITY

Inequality is acceptable even to egalitarians. Much depends on how it comes about. Consider a hypothetical problem: Two citizens, A and B, start off equal in some respect, each with, say $100. A year later, A has $200; B, none. Is B entitled to some, or all, of A's gain, to have, as it were, a condition of equality restored? Much depends, one might say, on how this came to pass. If B lost his money to A because of force or fraud, very likely so. But if B merely mislaid the money, while A gained more from someone else, that might be another story altogether.

The point is a simple one: What the fact of inequality signifies—what it says about the larger society, what remedies it requires, even whether it signifies a violation of the value of equality—depends on who or what is thought to be responsible for it. And it is, therefore, to the explanations Americans offer for the fact of inequality that we now turn.

MEASURING EXPLANATIONS

As part of both the National Election Study and the Bay Area Study, random samples of Americans were asked which of six reasons, as they saw it, explain the fact of racial inequality. The question put to them began this way:

> We've asked questions like this of quite a few people by now, both blacks and whites, and they have very different ideas about why, on the average, white people get more of

TABLE 2.1

Explanations for Racial Inequality

	National			Bay Area		
	% Agree	% Disagree	(N)	% Agree	% Disagree	(N)
1. A small group of powerful and wealthy white people control things and act to keep blacks down.	39	61	(918)	44	56	(662)
2. The differences are brought about by God; God made the races different as part of His divine plan.	55	45	(905)	39	61	(635)
3. It's really a matter of some people not trying hard enough; if blacks would only try harder, they could be just as well off as whites.	69	31	(930)	45	55	(663)
4. Generations of slavery and discrimination have created conditions that make it difficult for blacks to work their way out of the lower class.	72	28	(926)	78	22	(669)
5. Black Americans teach their children values and skills different from those required to be successful in American society.	52	48	(804)	49	51	(656)
6. Blacks come from a less able race and this explains why blacks are not as well off as whites in America.	31	69	(882)	23	77	(543)

the "good things in life" in America than black people. I
will read you some of the reasons people have given, including some things that other people don't agree with at all.[1]

What are the reasons for racial inequality, in the minds
of white Americans? Table 2.1 shows the percentage agreeing
with each of six reasons.[2] A person can agree with as many
of these reasons as he or she thinks make sense. The reasons
are not all the ones that could be given for blacks being worse
off; but they include many of those commonly given, and are,
all in all, quite various, ranging from economic exploitation
to lack of ability.

Of the six reasons presented, the one that makes sense to
the most people is the same in both studies. Seventy-two percent in the NES and 78 percent in the BAS agree that "generations of slavery and discrimination have created conditions that
make it difficult for blacks to work their way out of the lower
class." This explanation, we suspect, owes part of its popularity
to its vagueness; there is an obscurity, not so much about what
this line of reasoning asserts as about what it denies, a point
we later develop in detail.

If the two studies agree on the most popular explanation
of inequality, they also agree on the least popular: Blacks lack
ability. Sixty-nine percent of the national sample and 77 percent of the regional one disagree with the statement "Blacks
come from a less able race and this explains why blacks are
not as well off as whites in America." To put the point in its
most positive form, in both studies fewer than one white in
three agrees with this assertion of inherent racial inferiority.

Two quite different explanations each divide Americans
into nearly equal camps. In both samples, approximately one-
half agrees with the proposition that "black Americans teach
their children values and skills different from those required
to be successful in American society." Comparable in popularity
to this socialization explanation is one that centers on exploitation. Again in both samples, about four in ten white Americans
agree with the statement "A small group of powerful and wealthy
white people control things and act to keep blacks down."

But if the two samples are alike on these points, they are different on two others. In the country as a whole, a majority agrees that racial inequality has divine backing; in the Bay Area, a majority disagrees. Specifically, in the NES study, 55 percent agree with the statement "The differences [between races] are brought about by God; God made the races different as part of His divine plan." In contrast, in the BAS, only 39 percent agree.

The difference is not surprising. The San Francisco Bay Area is hardly representative of the country as a whole; it is distinctive in climate of opinion, life style, and political temper. Taking this into account, what strikes us as worth emphasis is the extraordinary number of people, even in the Bay Area, who find it sensible to ascribe the disadvantages that blacks suffer to divine command—a reminder of the tenacity of religious ideas even in a secular society.

A final explanation strikes a familiar chord. Why are blacks worse off than whites? Because they do not work as hard. This kind of reasoning is familiar not merely because it reproduces an old racial stereotype but because it expresses the kernel of popular theories of achievement. What does it take to succeed? Hard work, individual initiative, and perserverance. This is a very popular approach to understanding racial inequality. In the national sample, 69 percent agree with the statement "It's really a matter of some people not trying hard enough; if blacks would only try harder, they could be just as well off as whites." In the regional sample, 45 percent agree with this notion, a smaller proportion than in the country as a whole but a large number all the same.

Americans—90 percent of them in the NES—agree with more than one of these explanations. This is not surprising. Ask a thousand people a question, and some of them will have no idea what it is about. Ask them questions about the origins of racial inequality, and that will be more than a handful. The problem is not with those willing to admit that they do not understand the question or do not have an opinion to give in response to it. We know who they are. The difficulty arises because some people, precisely because they do not have anything really to say, are willing to say practically anything to avoid the embarrassment of appearing to be empty-headed or foolish. How shall we tell who they are? By taking advantage of their willingness to agree with a point of view, whether they really hold it or not, in order to give the impression of actually having one. To put the point differently, there is not often a need, when interviewing people about politics, to concoct some Machiavellian scheme to induce them to express an opinion. The problem, if anything, is the other way about: They are willing to offer an opinion even if they hold none. That is, it is precisely when people have nothing much to say that they are overly ready to say anything at all in order to appear as though they really do have something to say. Accordingly, to determine who holds a definite opinion about the reasons for racial inequality in America, we exclude all who, when presented with a reason, agree with it, whatever it is. In all, there are 120 respondents in the NES sample and 43 in the BAS sample who give themselves away by agreeing with all four of the questions we use here.

More fundamentally, racial inequality is a complex problem; it may have more than one cause and therefore more than one explanation. What we want to find out, then, is not what people think about each possible cause in isolation from their views about the others. To get a grip on their overall position, we need take account not only of their beliefs but also of their disbeliefs; we need to determine which factors they think are responsible for racial inequality—and which they think are not. When this is done, we can go deeper than we can by looking at each explanation separately; we can make out fundamental orientations toward the problem of inequality, orientations that reflect two major themes of American culture.

Two Themes

Benjamin Franklin, it has been remarked, is the "First American."[3] For Franklin marks the passage from a provincial consciousness to a continental, American, one. What is central to this consciousness? The values that Franklin extolled and that have come to be seen as distinctively American are these: self-reliance, achievement, perseverance, individual initiative, and independence. These virtues fit together, forming a theme in American life. Tocqueville wrote of Americans: "They owe nothing to any man; they expect nothing from any man. They acquire the habit of always considering themselves standing alone." Tocqueville's counterpart in the nineteenth century, James Bryce, joined in, remarking that in America, "everything tends to make the individual independent and self-reliant."[4]

This theme—this ethic of self-reliance, as we call it—is familiar still. It finds expression, for example, in the notion that everyone should stand on his or her own two feet, that success is not a matter of luck or fate but of talent and effort, that people should take care of their own problems themselves.[5] The ethic of self-reliance may not be as strong or as pervasive now as it was one hundred or two hundred years ago. Many conservatives complain of its loss, though the popularity of their lamentations may be proof of its tenacity. At all events, studies focusing on the core values of equality and achievement and on an array of character traits—personal efficacy, conformism, optimism, and the like—have emphasized the continuity of belief in the American experience, of which the ethic of self-reliance is an integral part.[6]

A second theme of the American ethos has been moralism. Gunnar Myrdal, perhaps the most penetrating foreign observer of American values in this century, has written: "It must be observed that America, relative to all the other branches of Western civilization, is moralistic and 'moral-conscious.' "[7] This moralism shows itself in the readiness of Americans to scrutinize, to criticize, to reproach, not just others, but themselves as well—indeed, perhaps particularly themselves and their institutions. Myrdal may have exaggerated in speaking of an "American eagerness to get on record one's sins and their causes."[8] Not by much, however, as post-Watergate America has shown again.

Of course, self-criticism is not confined to Americans. What makes moralism a distinctively American political style is its ambivalence about America. At one level America is the promised land. "We Americans," Melville trumpeted, "are the peculiar, chosen people—the Israel of our time; we bear the ark of the liberties of the world."[9] But if at one level there is affirmation, at another there is denunciation. What is America? "The world's fairest hope," Melville answered, "linked with man's foulest crime."[10]

It is this kind of moralism—set apart by its readiness to condemn, not merely to criticize—on which we want to focus. If this moralistic strain is apparent in the American experience, it is particularly so in the history of American responses to the issue of racial inequality.[11]

These two themes—self-reliance and moralism—seem to be integral parts of the American ethos. The two are, of course, themselves related, a point Tocqueville made in his hyperbolic declaration that the "whole destiny of America is contained in the first Puritan who landed on these shores, as that of the whole human race in the first man."[12] But the two concepts are distinguishable analytically. Taken separately, each characterizes a fundamental axis in American ideas about inequality; put together, the two capture major cleavages in the ways that Americans explain why blacks have less than whites.

A Typology

Imagine these two themes—self-reliance and moralism—as independent dimensions of American political culture, as shown in figure 2.1 on page 36. The two dimensions define a fourfold typology. In speaking of different orientations to inequality, we do not at all mean to suggest that Americans are divided into four mental species, each distinct and immutable, depending on their outlook toward inequality. Rather, the purpose of our typology is to exaggerate, and so make palpable, tendencies that might otherwise be obscured given the crudity of measurement techniques. Our classificatory scheme is a device of convenience, a means of identifying flesh-and-blood examples of abstract ideas, of seeing, for example, what a person who believes in individualism looks and thinks like. For our ultimate aim is to use interviews with individual Americans, conducted

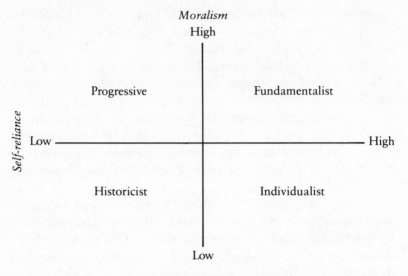

Moralism
High

Progressive   Fundamentalist

Low ———————————————————————————————— High

Historicist   Individualist

Low

FIGURE 2.1
Two Dimensions

at one point in time, as a mirror, to catch in their ideas and
points of view reflections of fundamental themes of the American ethos itself.

The first orientation toward inequality, in the lower right
quadrant of figure 2.1, is the individualist. In general terms,
this is an outlook that emphasizes individual responsibility
above all. The individualist, on the one side, says blacks are
worse off because they do not apply themselves as they should,
and on the other, denies blacks are worse off because powerful
and wealthy whites keep them down.[13] One can see how accepting the one idea and rejecting the other constitute a whole: an
affirmation of the principle of individual responsibility.

A second orientation, in the upper left quadrant of figure
2.1, is the progressive. The mirror image of the individualist
outlook, it emphasizes moralism. This second way of looking
at inequality represents blacks not as failures but as victims.
A progressive is a person who blames wealthy and powerful
whites for keeping blacks down and simultaneously rejects the
suggestion that blacks bear the onus for their situation in life
for not trying as hard as they could and should to improve it.[14]

A third orientation is the fundamentalist.[15] Its core, of course, is an insistence on a religious rather than a secular explanation of racial inequality.[16] In the American context, a religious perspective on public affairs is likely to be a moralistic one. But if it is clear where fundamentalism falls on the vertical dimension, where it is located on the horizontal—self-reliance—is less obvious. In the past, fundamentalism and activist liberalism have been allies.[17] But since the 1920s the dominant tendency has been for fundamentalism to go together with belief in individual responsibility. Accordingly, we have placed it in the upper right quadrant.[18]

Finally, there is historicism. This is an approach to understanding inequality that is as significantly defined by the kind of reasoning it rejects as by the kind it accepts. It is a way of explaining present inequality in terms of the past—specifically, generations of slavery and discrimination. But a purely historicist perspective not only acknowledges that the past makes a difference; it rejects alternative explanations. And the person who labels racial inequality a historical wrong and does not hold somebody responsible for it now—whether society, God, or blacks themselves—we call historicist.[19]

We can measure the popularity, in the country as a whole and in the Bay Area, of competing orientations to inequality. Figure 2.2 on page 38 presents the percentages favoring each of the four explanatory modes—historicist, progressive, individualist, and fundamentalist—in the NES and BAS surveys.[20]

The most popular mode of explanation for racial inequality, in the country as a whole, is the individualist: Blacks have less of the good things in life because they do not try hard enough, not because rich whites keep them down. Nationally, this is the position of a clear majority of white Americans.

As figure 2.2 shows, it is a less popular position in the Bay Area. There, 35 percent of the respondents are individualist, compared to 57 percent in the whole country. That "old-fashioned" individualism is comparatively less popular in a liberal climate of opinion like the Bay Area is not surprising. And considering how liberal the Bay Area is, perhaps the lesson to draw is that individualism has remarkable tenacity; for even there,

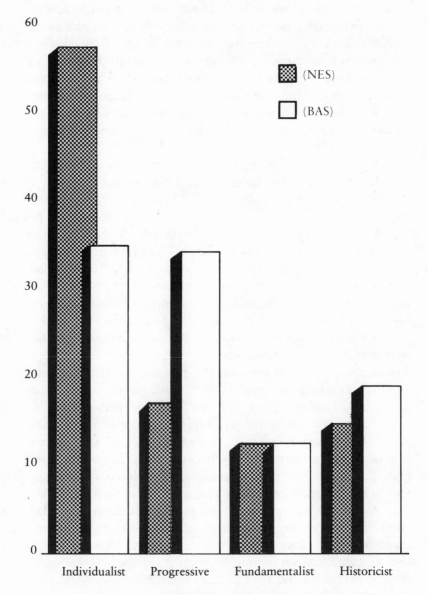

FIGURE 2.2
Modes of Explanation for Racial Inequality (in percent)

no other explanation for inequality is more popular than the individualist.

The difference in temper between this politically charged area and the country as a whole shows up strikingly in the popularity of the progressive orientation. One-third of the BAS respondents see racial inequality as a product of exploitation, compared to 17 percent in the NES. With respect to the two remaining modes of explanation—fundamentalist and historicist—the two samples present much the same picture. About one in six attributes the disadvantages of blacks to past discrimination and slavery—and to no other factor. And in both samples, 12 percent, or about one in eight, see in the burdens under which blacks labor evidence of divine justice.

DEMOGRAPHIC CORRELATES OF EXPLANATORY MODES

Education

The ideas of those who know the least tend to be ideas that are known best. The person with a lot of education is likely to know something of the stream of new ideas circulating through the society. In contrast, the one with little schooling is drawn to ideas that are "traditional," not necessarily because of any desire to uphold tradition, but because long-standing ideas tend to be familiar ideas. Character—the importance of trying hard, of showing individual initiative—is a commonplace of the popular culture; so is religion. Both ways of explaining inequality accordingly appeal most to those with the least education.

Table 2.2 on page 40 shows that this is the case. Fundamentalists have had the least education; next to them, individualists. In the national sample, one-half of the fundamentalists and one-third of the individualists did not complete high school. Conversely, historicists tended to be quite well educated, while progressives finished a close second. Thus, one in three of the former, and one in four of the latter, have graduated from college, compared to only one in ten individualists or fundamentalists.

TABLE 2.2
Education (in percent)

	Individualist (NES)	(BAS)	Progressive (NES)	(BAS)	Fundamentalist (NES)	(BAS)	Historicist (NES)	(BAS)
No high school	16	7	12	3	27	9	5	2
Some high school	17	14	9	9	21	9	5	1
High school graduates	40	34	31	24	30	38	27	30
Some college	17	25	24	25	13	27	25	25
College graduates	10	21	24	40	9	18	37	43
(N)	(392)	(191)	(121)	(187)	(86)	(68)	(95)	(105)

NOTE: In both samples, p is less than .05.

In the northern California sample, in the context of a more educated population, the pattern is the same. Given that people living in the Bay Area are twice as likely as the national population to have a college degree, the similarity between the national and the Bay Area figures is impressive. Again, historicists and progressives are the best educated: 43 percent of the former and 40 percent of the latter completed college. And again fundamentalists and individualists have had the least schooling. Indeed, in the Bay Area, where 48 percent of whites have attended or completed college, one-fifth of the fundamentalists and individualists failed to finish high school.

Age

One may look at American ideas of equality in terms of socialization, not merely schooling. Citizens acquire some of their basic political orientations when they are young. Political partisanship is an example of this; ideas about racial inequality may be as well. For they embody assumptions about what is right, natural, proper; they are the sort of assumptions many acquire as children, then carry with them as adults. To the extent that this is so, much of what Americans believe about racial inequality now reflects what their parents and their parents' generation believed.

On this reasoning, traditional explanations of inequality— that is, fundamentalist and individualist—should appeal most to older Americans. For these outlooks were, in all probability, even more prevalent a generation ago than they are now. Modernist explanations—historicist and progressive—should appeal more to the younger, that is, those who were children as American culture was becoming more secular and liberal.

As figure 2.3 shows, the relationship between age and explanations for inequality broadly fits our expectations. In both surveys, fundamentalists and individualists are oldest (though the order as between the two varies with the survey). Historicists are plainly younger than either, and progressives younger still, particularly in the Bay Area. This finding may be taken as a further indication that ideas about inequality reflect to a degree a cleavage between traditional and modernist outlooks.

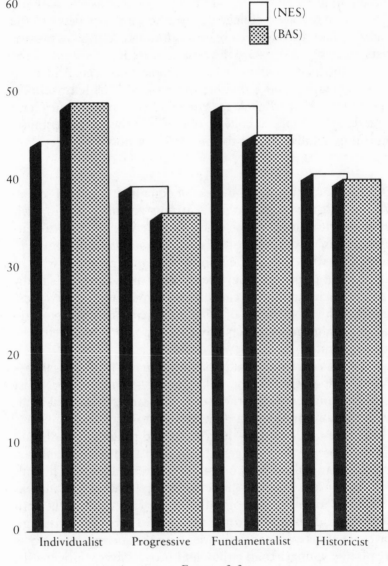

FIGURE 2.3
Age (average)

NOTE: In both samples, p is less than .05.

Gender

If we expected to find a connection between age and orientation toward inequality, the same was not true about gender. There is no theoretical reason to suppose that one orientation would appeal especially to women, another to men. Yet figure 2.4 on page 44 shows that there is indeed such a connection in the case of fundamentalism. In the national sample, somewhat more than half of the respondents being analyzed (57 percent) are women. In contrast, 69 percent of the fundamentalists are women. Moreover, this disparity is even more pronounced in the Bay Area survey; there, 82 percent of the fundamentalists are women. None of the other orientations toward inequality is consistently linked to gender; and we should say frankly that we are not sure what to make of the finding that fundamentalism is.[21] Perhaps it suffices to observe that this relationship, though significant, is by no means strong. By comparison, education is many times more important in shaping ideas about inequality than gender.

Region

Where Americans were born likely matters too. On some political issues this may no longer be as true as it was two or three generations ago. But when it comes to the politics of race, North and South, for all their common problems, represent different climates of belief.

Given our sense of what these explanatory modes represent as mental outlooks, we would expect to find that traditional orientations are more prevalent in the South. And, on examination, the facts are as common sense led us to expect. As figure 2.5 on page 45 shows, fundamentalists, and next to them individualists, are the most likely to live in the South; progressives and historicists are the least likely.[22]

Income

Is there any connection, it is natural to ask, between how whites explain why blacks are not well-off and how well-off they themselves are? Are those who are successful—at least in terms of income—likely to account for blacks' lack of success in differ-

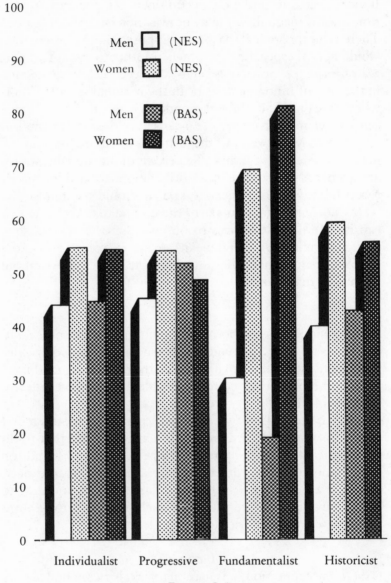

100

90

80

70

60

50

40

30

20

10

0

Men ☐ (NES)

Women ▦ (NES)

Men ▦ (BAS)

Women ▩ (BAS)

Individualist   Progressive   Fundamentalist   Historicist

FIGURE 2.4
Gender (in percent)

NOTE: In the NES, *p* is less than .10. In the BAS, *p* is less than .05.

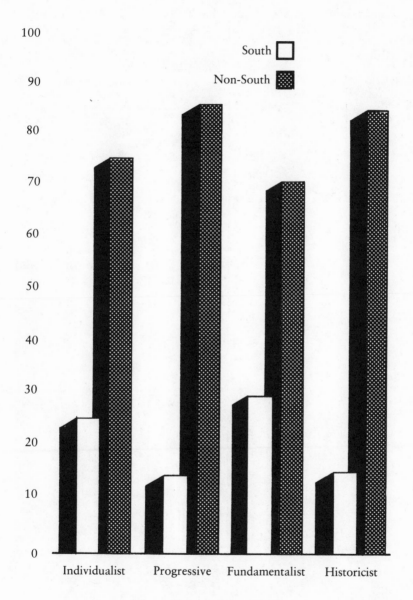

100

90

80

70

60

50

40

30

20

10

0

South ☐
Non-South ▨

Individualist   Progressive   Fundamentalist   Historicist

FIGURE 2.5
Region (in percent)

NOTE: *p* is less than .05.

TABLE 2.3
Income (in percent)

	Individualist (NES)	(BAS)	Progressive (NES)	(BAS)	Fundamentalist (NES)	(BAS)	Historicist (NES)	(BAS)
Less than $5000	18	10	18	18	32	18	17	4
$5000-$9,999	36	26	33	22	35	20	19	16
$10,000-$15,000	24	23	20	27	17	32	22	30
More than $15,000	23	42	29	33	16	30	42	51
(N)	(384)	(179)	(116)	(181)	(82)	(66)	(93)	(101)

NOTE: In both samples, *p* is less than .05.

ent ways than those who have had less success? Table 2.3 compares the annual earnings (in 1972) of each of the explanatory modes. Historicists are easily the best-off. In the national study, 42 percent of them made $15,000 or more; in the regional study, 51 percent of them did so. At the other end of the scale are the fundamentalists. They are the most poorly off in the BAS, with a fifth of them making less than $5000; even more obviously so in the NES, with a third of them making less than $5000. And in between historicists and fundamentalists are the individualists and, more equivocally, the progressives.[23]

The relation between individualism and income calls for further comment. Individualism, it has been argued, is a success ethic.[24] Indeed, it attaches so much importance to getting ahead as to equate individual achievement and personal worth. Given this pressure to succeed, those who fail feel their self-esteem, their self-respect, threatened. To salvage their sense of self-worth, they persuade themselves that "they are not the failures that they might have been and that others—for want of effort and competence—are."[25] The trick, then, is to compare oneself with others who have done still less well. From this angle, one may seem to have done comparatively well, even though one's achievements have fallen short of one's aspirations. And whom better with which to compare oneself than blacks? The very fact that they have less is a measure that they have done less—presumably a balm for the white American who has not done well but who can feel himself or herself a modest personal success compared with striking black failure.

This reading of individualism as a strategy the unsuccessful use for psychological defense is a popular one, particularly among critics of individualism. Our analysis, however, suggests that individualism and income are not related: Whether or not a person attributes blacks' lack of success to a lack of effort has nothing to do with how much money he or she earns.[26]

Social Class
Income is one measure of a person's place in American society; social class is another. By class we mean a person's perception of his or her social position; specifically, whether one per-

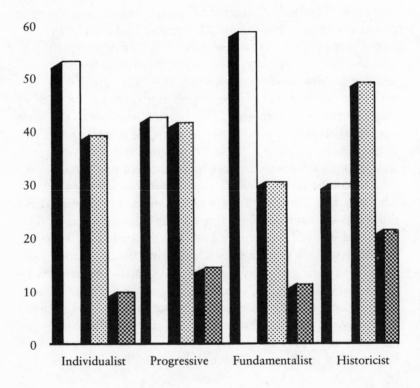

FIGURE 2.6
Social Class (NES) (in percent)

NOTE: *p* is less than .05.

ceives oneself as middle class, in one degree or another, or working class.

Figure 2.6 on page 48 reports the relation between the four explanatory modes and class identification. Individualists and fundamentalists tend to be working class, while progressives and historicists more often tend to be middle or upper-middle class. This is particularly obvious in the case of the historicist. Otherwise, the differences, though visible, are modest.

Looking at the relation between class identification and type of explanation from the opposite angle, working-class respondents are more likely to be individualists, middle-class ones less so, upper-middle-class ones still less so (though in every stratum individualism is the most popular view). This indicates how misleading the expression "middle-class values" can be. For the point to understand about many so-called middle-class values is precisely that they are not confined to any one class or segment of the society. Quite the contrary. They tend to be pervasive, enjoying broad support throughout the society and underlining the hegemony of a popular, not a class, culture.[27]

A POLITICAL PROFILE: IDEOLOGY AND OPINION

The most popular mode of explanation for racial inequality, in the minds of white Americans, is character—or, rather, a lack thereof; blacks have less of the "good things in life" than whites because they try less than whites. This explanation invokes a distinctively American theory of achievement—a theory that has entered the popular culture in the figure of Horatio Alger. And by paying particular attention to this theme of individualism—of the decisive importance of individual effort, initiative, perseverance, and character—we hope to throw light on the conservative ambivalence of a liberal tradition.

For individualism so understood is an idea of the political right. Its conservative temper is evident in figure 2.7 on page 50, which illustrates the extent to which people who subscribe to the various explanations of inequality have a distinctive point of view on some major political issues.

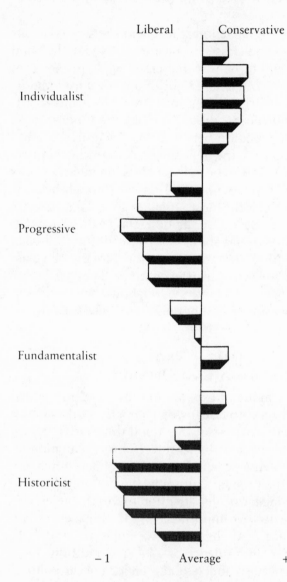

Liberal   Conservative

Individualist

                                  Guaranteed Jobs
                                  Rights of Accused
                                  Aid to Minorities
                                  Urban Unrest
                                  Lib./Con.

Guaranteed Jobs
Rights of Accused
Progressive — Aid to Minorities
Urban Unrest
Lib./Con.

Guaranteed Jobs
Rights of Accused
Fundamentalist — Aid to Minorities
Urban Unrest
Lib./Con.

Guaranteed Jobs
Rights of Accused
Historicist — Aid to Minorities
Urban Unrest
Lib./Con.

− 1   Average   + 1

FIGURE 2.7
Ideology and Opinion (NES)

NOTE: On all measures, *p* is less than .05.

The issues cover a range of concerns: whether the government in Washington should see to it that every person has a job and a good standard of living or just let each person get ahead on his or her own; whether it is more important to protect the legal rights of those accused of crime or to stop criminal activity even at the risk of reducing the rights of the accused; whether the government in Washington should make every possible effort to improve the social and economic position of blacks and other minorities or should not make any special effort to help minorities because they should help themselves; and whether it is more important to use all available force to maintain law and order in dealing with urban riots and unrest or to correct the problems of poverty and unemployment that give rise to disturbances. Also, respondents were asked to indicate how liberal or conservative they are, as they themselves understand these terms. In sum, we have measures both of what people believe and of what they believe that they believe; the two may be easily confused—a confusion, we suggest, that helps explain both the strength and incoherence of the right in America.

For each issue, opposing positions define the endpoints of a seven-point scale; everyone is invited to indicate his or her view of the issue by picking a number on the scale. In figure 2.7, the solid vertical line expresses the average position people chose on each issue.[28]

Individualists are clearly conservative; only they are on the right, politically and graphically, on the issue of government guarantees for jobs and standard of living. The same goes for the issue of law and order; forced to choose between protecting the rights of those accused of crime and stopping crime, only the individualists are to the right of the average. The problem of urban riots reflects another facet of this law-and-order stance; here, too, the position of the individualists is distinctively conservative. They are also on the political right with respect to government programs for blacks and other minorities, though fundamentalists, too, are less than enthusiastic about programs of this sort. And not only do individualists take conservative positions; they think of themselves as conservative, as figure 2.7 makes plain.[29]

TABLE 2.4
Ideology and Opinion (NES)

	Individualist	Progressive	Fundamentalist	Historicist
Guaranteed Jobs	.27	−.36	−.36	−.30
Rights of Accused	.49	−.69	−.07	−.97
Aid to Minorities	.46	−.86	.26	−.91
Urban Unrest	.42	−.61	0	−.84
Lib./Con. Ideology	.29	−.56	.23	−.50

NOTE: On all measures, *p* is less than .05.

This is in sharp contrast to the progressives and historicists; their center of gravity, politically, is plainly to the left. Moreover, in terms of what they actually believe, not merely what they believe that they believe, progressives and historicists are liberal—for all practical purposes equally so, possibly not in every respect but certainly in terms of the core issues considered here. On all these issues, the views of both veer to the left of those of the (mathematically) average American. So both progressives and historicists, to cite an especially striking result, distinguish themselves in support of the view that government should make every effort to improve the social and economic position of blacks and other minorities. In sum, not only do progressives and historicists have a definite point of view politically—on the left—but they know what it is.

It is tempting, then, to suggest that there is an ideological divide: modernist explanations of inequality on the political left, traditional on the right. But the fundamentalists show that no simple liberal/conservative, modern/traditional cleavage captures the complexity, and the confusion, of real life. For fundamentalists both are and are not conservative.

Fundamentalists see themselves as belonging on the right.[30] And in terms of their political likes and dislikes, fundamentalists are conservative: They are as positive or warm in their feelings toward conservatives, and as negative or cool toward liberals, as the individualists. Finally, on issues of morals— legalization of marijuana or abortion—they are, if anything, to the right of the individualists.[31]

All of this is true and important; yet on a range of issues the fundamentalists, far from being on the far right, are in the center or even to the left of it. So with respect to controlling urban unrest, the views of fundamentalists surely do not resemble the war cries of law-and-order conservatives. The same is true on the issue of protecting the rights of the accused. To be sure, the views of fundamentalists do have a conservative coloration on the issue of government aid for blacks. But what is telling is the reaction of fundamentalists to the issue most symbolic of New Deal liberalism: whether government has a responsibility to see that citizens can work and have a decent standard of living. Fundamentalists, far from rallying to the conservative banner, take a comparatively liberal stand on government jobs. Indeed, on this issue, their views and those of progressives and historicists are, quite simply, indistinguishable.

There is, then, something of a discrepancy between what fundamentalists believe and what they believe that they believe. And to the extent that they act on the basis of what they think that they think, the mass appeal of the political right is broadened beyond the programmatically conservative camp. The significance of the intersection of Christian fundamentalism and right-wing politics, then, is this: Fundamentalist moralism gives the political right a chance to secure a liberal following.

TRADITIONAL VERSUS NONTRADITIONAL

An official theme of American culture is innovation, openness to experience. Illustrations of this theme abound in familiar clichés of the popular culture: in the importance of progress; in pioneer themes; in the popular sense of America as a society of achievement, implicitly to be distinguished from older societies of ascription, custom, and tradition. And in a culture that is in some important sense defined by opposition to tradition, it is worth remarking one of the forms that traditionalism takes: anti-intellectualism.

Anti-intellectualism has been a major theme in American politics.[32] The portrait of intellectuals in American culture presents them as "pretentious, conceited, effeminate, and snobbish; and very likely immoral, dangerous, and subversive."[33] The intellectual, so conceived, offends against common sense — and the common man. The intellectual makes a claim to superior knowledge, and so to superiority itself.

This suspicion and resentment of intellectualism can be captured in the NES study. For among the questions asked were these:[34]

1. I prefer the practical man anytime to the man of ideas.
2. People ought to pay more attention to new ideas, even if they seem to go against the American way of life.

54

Anti-intellectualism so conceived consists in a prejudice for ideas that have, in the common expression, stood the test of time, and against new ideas, or ideas that are threatening because they are unfamiliar or at odds with received opinion. Anti-intellectualism, then, is one aspect of conservatism and, as such, an element common to the mental outlook of both individualists and fundamentalists—or so we would hypothesize.

Figure 2.8 on page 56 shows the connection between anti-intellectualism and explanatory modes. The results are clear-cut: The two modes of accounting for inequality that are traditional in American culture—the individualist and the fundamentalist—both score high on the Anti-Intellectualism Index; the other two modes both score low.[35]

This we take to be one more illustration of the protean character of the notion of equality. For the point to appreciate about traditionalism when it takes the form of anti-intellectualism, as here, is that it is a populistic argument against privilege. It is populist because it is anti-elitist, for intellectuals mark themselves a cut above the common man. And to be skeptical of new ideas, of science even, is to argue against a secret knowledge, restricted to the few, subversive of the convictions of the many. Anti-intellectualism has its roots in a religious tradition that is, in Hofstadter's expression, "evangellically egalitarian"[36]—hence its appeal to the fundamentalist—and in a cultural tradition that is populistically self-reliant—hence its appeal to the individualist. In a word, in the American experience, anti-intellectualism may be a form of vulgar egalitarianism.

CONCLUSION

The cleavage, it would seem, is between the individualist and fundamentalist on the one side, and the progressive and historicist on the other. The former have in common a more traditional temper, the latter a more modernist one. But, as we see in the next chapter, the progressive and the fundamentalist—two groups that could hardly be more dissimilar in social circumstance and political ideology—share a similar animus: moralism.

+1

High

Average

Low

−1

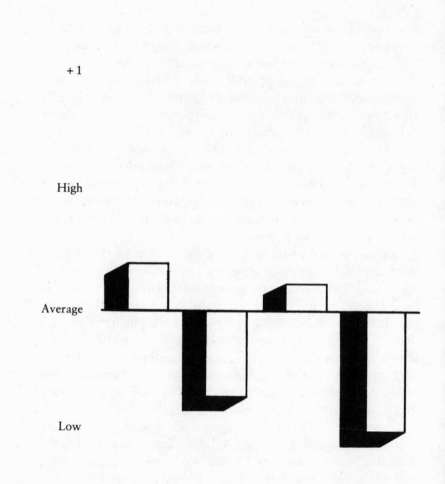

Individualist   Progressive   Fundamentalist   Historicist

FIGURE 2.8
Anti-Intellectualism, Controlling Education (NES)

NOTE: *p* is less than .05.

NOTES

1. The question takes the fact of racial inequality as a given. We take the fact that people were, by and large, willing to answer the question as evidence that respondents, too, accept that premise. In both surveys, 98 percent of those presented with the six reasons for inequality agreed with at least one of them.
2. The actual question format had four response alternatives: *agree a great deal, agree somewhat, disagree somewhat,* and *disagree a great deal.* No explicit "don't know" alternative was presented. To simplify presentation, these categories have been collapsed into *agree* and *disagree.*
3. Yehoshua Arieli, *Individualism and Nationalism in American Ideology* (Baltimore: Penguin, 1964), 43.
4. We are indebted for the general point, and for these particular quotations, to Alex Inkeles, "Continuity and Change in American National Character," in *The Third Century: America as a Post-Industrial Society,* ed. Seymour Martin Lipset (Chicago: University of Chicago Press, 1979).
5. Our interest in this ethic of self-reliance stems from earlier work done with Richard Brody. See Richard A. Brody and Paul M. Sniderman, "From Life Space to Polling Place," *British Journal of Political Science* 7 (1977): 337-60; and Paul M. Sniderman and Richard A. Brody, "Coping: The Ethic of Self-Reliance," *American Journal of Political Science* 21 (1977): 501-21.
6. Seymour Martin Lipset, *The First New Nation: The United States in Historical and Comparative Perspective* (New York: Norton, 1979); and Inkeles, "Continuity and Change in American National Character."
7. Gunnar Myrdal, *An American Dilemma: The Negro Problem and Modern Democracy* (New York: Harper & Bros., 1944), xlvi. See also Samuel P. Huntington, *American Politics: The Promise of Disharmony* (Cambridge, Mass.: Harvard University Press, 1981).
8. Myrdal, *An American Dilemma,* 22.
9. Quoted in Sacvan Bercovitch, *The American Jeremiad* (Madison: University of Wisconsin Press, 1978), 177.
10. Quoted in ibid., 194.
11. Stanley Elkins, cited in Huntington, *American Politics,* 112.
12. Quoted in Bercovitch, *The American Jeremiad,* 7.
13. Operationally, then, an individualist is one who agrees with the third explanation in table 2.1 and disagrees with the first.
14. Operationally, the progressive is one who agrees with the first explanaion in table 2.1 and disagrees with the third.
15. Throughout, our investigation of the fundamentalist explanation for equality has been greatly aided by John J. Hansen, "The Fundamentalist Personality" (Honors thesis, Department of Political Science, Stanford University, 1981).
16. Those with a fundamentalist orientation were extracted from among those

with neither an individualist nor a progressive orientation. Operationally, a fundamentalist is one who agrees with the second explanation in table 2.1 and disagrees with the first and the third.

17. For an especially sensitive and instructive account, on which we have relied at various points in our analysis, see George M. Marsden, *Fundamentalism and American Culture* (New York: Oxford University Press, 1980).

18. See chapter 3 for a discussion of some of the elements responsible for the political ambiguity of so-called right-wing fundamentalism.

19. Operationally, an historicist is one who agrees with the fourth explanation in table 2.1 and disagrees with the first three.

20. Defined in this way, our typology includes 65 percent of those asked to explain inequality in the NES survey, 57 percent of those in the BAS survey.

21. We have examined a number of factors, such as education and religiosity, to test for spuriousness, without success.

22. The South, as defined here, includes Alabama, Arkansas, Florida, Georgia, Louisiana, Mississippi, North Carolina, South Carolina, Texas, and Virginia.

23. More equivocally, we say, because in the Bay Area the progressives earn the same as fundamentalists; however, this impression of similarity is misleading, given the enormous difference between them in age in the BAS.

24. For an especially thorough presentation of this line of argument, see Michael Lewis, *The Culture of Inequality* (Amherst: University of Massachusetts Press, 1978).

25. Ibid., 43.

26. See chapter 3 for a showing that individualism is *not* associated with low self-esteem.

27. In this connection, it is well to remark Schlozman and Verba's provocative hypothesis on the increasing homogeneity of the popular values, at least as captured in the American dream. See Kay Lehman Schlozman and Sidney Verba, *Injury to Insult: Unemployment, Class, and Political Response* (Cambridge, Mass.: Harvard University Press, 1979), chap. 5.

28. Table 2.4 reproduces the results of figure 2.7. There are two reasons for this. The first is the complexity of figure 2.7, given the number of variables displayed. The second is a desire on our part to provide an example of the numerical results yielded by Multiple Classification Analysis (MCA), the analytic technique employed throughout the remainder of this book. For a brief discussion of MCA, see appendix C.

29. Both of the studies include measures of ideological self-identification; even though the wording of the questions is different, the results are virtually identical. The text of the question in the NES study was as follows:

Explanations for Racial Inequality

We hear a lot of talk these days about liberals and conservatives. I'm going to show you a seven-point scale on which the political views that people might hold are arranged from extremely liberal to extremely conservative. Where would you place yourself on this scale, or haven't you thought much about this?

The text of the question in the BAS study was:

In politics, would you say that you are a radical, a liberal, a conservative, a strong conservative, or would you call yourself middle-of-the-road?

In the NES study, 43 percent of the individualists label themselves conservatives; in the BAS, 40 percent. In the NES study, 40 percent of the historicists and 52 percent of the progressives describe themselves as liberals; in the BAS, 48 percent of the former and 44 percent of the latter.

30. In both the NES and the BAS, the result is the same: fundamentalists are twice as likely to describe themselves as conservative than as liberal.
31. Data not shown.
32. We rely here on Richard Hofstadter's classic analysis, *Anti-Intellectualism in American Life* (New York: Vintage Books, 1962).
33. Ibid., 19.
34. The model for our measure was Miller and Levitin's measure of traditionalism. Their measure contained a third item, which dealt with the conflict between religion and science. This item was omitted to avoid a misleading impression of dissimilarity between individualists and fundamentalists. For a full description of their procedure, see Warren E. Miller and Teresa E. Levitin, *Leadership and Change: The New Politics and the American Electorate* (Cambridge, Mass.: Winthrop, 1976). For an explanation of our coding and scoring rules, see appendix B.
35. This figure shows scores on the Index controlling the effects of education.
36. Hofstadter, *Anti-Intellectualism in American Life*.

CHAPTER 3

MORALISM

Inequality raises issues of right and wrong. Why *should* blacks have less of the good things in life than whites? For many it is hard to respond to such a question without wanting to see a wrong as evidence of wrongdoing, without wishing to accuse, to blame, to judge, even to condemn. Moral issues invite moralistic responses; and moralism, as we shall see, is a habit of mind that unites two opposing views of inequality: the progressive and the fundamentalist.

THE SPIRIT OF MORALISM

The progressive and the fundamentalist embody not merely differing but clashing outlooks. The progressive comes from educated, young, liberal circles, the fundamentalist from the ranks of the poorly educated, the older, the conservative. And yet both outlooks — progressive and fundamentalist — share a common animus.

To see why this may be so, a word needs to be said about moralistic outlooks. View the world from a judgmental angle, and the people around you do not appear in a flattering light. For the emphasis of a moralizing style is on weakness, vanity, and greed — imperfection in all its human forms.[1] The language of sin and sinners comes easily to a fundamentalist, who maintains that God Himself has consigned blacks to a place of inferiority. But much the same point of view is taken by the person who blames racial inequality on exploitation by wealthy whites. For what counts is not the particular words used to denounce others, but the readiness to condemn them, to see them as different and unworthy of esteem or respect.

In contrast, historicism is a mental outlook defined by a refusal to indulge in moralizing; the historicist will blame neither black nor white for racial inequality. But then, one may ask, is it inappropriate to blame someone or something for racial inequality? Is the refusal of the historicist to do so perhaps a sign of complacency, of a refusal to take the fact of racial inequality seriously and personally? After all, race has been the American dilemma. There has been a flat contradiction, for any believer in the American creed, between the way that blacks have been treated and the way that they should be treated. And surely, asked why blacks are worse off than whites, it is understandable if people raise questions of responsibility, not to the exclusion of causes of inequality, but as part of an informed consideration of the complex of issues—moral as well as social—raised by the problem of inequality.

Moreover, is it altogether certain that individualism is itself not a form of moralism? Surely it is at least possible that individualists are being moralistic in insisting that the responsibility for blacks having less is their own. What we need to do, in short, is to get some sense of the spirit of different viewpoints on inequality, in particular of the extent to which they are hostile or judgmental. The telling consideration, then, is the attitude toward other people that characterizes each explanatory mode. A moralistic, accusatory style has a particular appeal, one would expect, to a person persuaded other people are, in general, not worthy of trust. For one mark of moralism is a readiness to believe that people are selfish, mean-spirited, and quick to take advantage. A moralist is precisely a person willing to put his or her faith in a higher idea but not in another human being.

It is necessary, then, to see who believes people are trustworthy and who does not. The NES contains three questions explicitly designed for this purpose:

1. Generally speaking, would you say that most people can be trusted, or that you can't be too careful in dealing with people?

2. Would you say that most of the time people try to be helpful, or that they are mostly just looking out for themselves?

3. Do you think most people would try to take advantage of you if they got a chance, or would they try to be fair?

These questions were combined to form an Index of Trust in People.[2] The lower the score on this Index, the less trust the person has in others—that is to say, the more misanthropic he or she is. As historicists resist moralizing, we would expect them to have faith in people. And as progressives and fundamentalists share a moralizing animus, we would expect them to have a misanthropic view of other people. To expect progressives and fundamentalists, we should emphasize, to be similar in this respect—indeed, in any respect—is certainly not to expect the obvious. For progressives tend to be liberal, fundamentalists conservative. And according to previous research, liberals tend to have high trust in people, conservatives low.[3]

Figure 3.1 on page 66 shows the connection between an individual's impression of whether other people are trustworthy or not and the way in which he or she accounts for racial inequality. To judge from the results, those who place their faith in God do not place their faith in their fellow citizens: Fundamentalists are the lowest on the Trust in People Index. The highest are the historicists, while the individualists are average, neither high nor low. And the progressives? They resemble the fundamentalists, falling below the average on the Trust Index. The resemblance is hardly exact; but, of course, fundamentalists are less well educated than progressives. And the less schooling that a person has had, the more readily he or she can be gulled into agreeing with oversimplified, derogatory remarks—sentiments that a well-educated person is more likely to recognize as being socially undesirable to express in the course of an interview.

Hence it is necessary to remove any impact of education and then look at the connection between trust in people and explanatory mode.

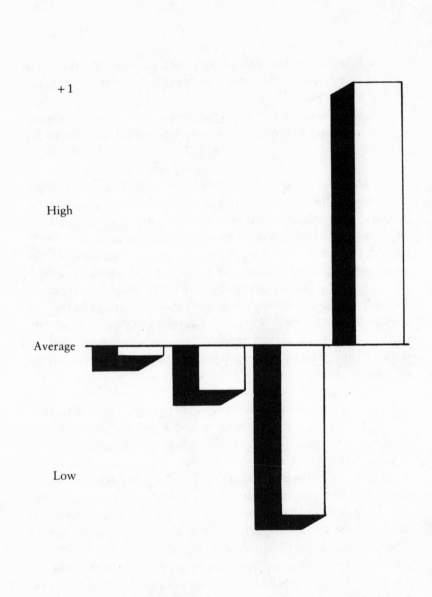

+ 1

High

Average

Low

− 1

Individualist   Progressive   Fundamentalist   Historicist

FIGURE 3.1
Trust in People (NES)

NOTE: *p* is less than .05.

These connections are shown in figure 3.2 on page 68. Now the resemblance between fundamentalists and progressives is much closer. The former are still misanthropic, but less so than it seemed at first; their lack of schooling, in addition to their religiosity, lowered their score. The latter are lacking in trust in people, and more plainly so after taking into account their better schooling. In short, set aside the extraneous question of education, and both fundamentalists and progressives show themselves to be, in temper and outlook, misanthropic.

Individualists, it is worth observing, are average on the Trust in People Index; they are not uncommonly generous in their opinion of others, but neither are they uncommonly mean-spirited. This is an instance of where failing to observe a relation can be as instructive as observing one. For the absence of any connection between misanthropy and individualism is a strong clue as to what the spirit of individualism is *not*. Although individualists do not have as much trust in people as historicists do, they have more than the frankly moralistic progressives and fundamentalists.

SELF-VALUATION

To what extent are ways of approaching as basic and provocative an issue as racial inequality drawn from an individual's sense of self—from inner needs, anxieties, and conflicts? Broadly stated, our idea is this: To the degree that interpretations of inequality serve to mobilize anger or express indignation, to that extent deeper reaches of an individual's psychological makeup are likely to be tapped.

There are not many measures of personality or quasi-personality traits in either the national or the regional study. There is, however, evidence on a key aspect of psychological makeup: self-valuation. In fact, two measures of self-valuation are available. One is personal competence—that is, the extent to which a person feels in control of his or her own life, able to plan ahead, confident of coping. A second is self-esteem—that is, the extent to which people feel themselves to be worthwhile and worthy of respect.[4]

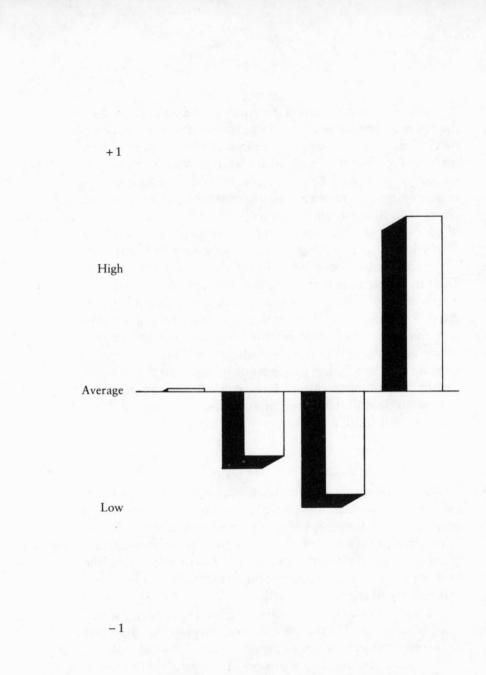

+1

High

Average

Low

−1

Individualist   Progressive   Fundamentalist   Historicist

FIGURE 3.2
Trust in People, Controlling Education (NES)

NOTE: *p* is less than .05.

We have, then, two independent tests of the moralist temperament—independent in several senses. The psychological qualities each assesses, though similar, are not the same. Moreover, one measure was used in the national study and the other in the regional one. This means that we have independent samples as well as independent indicators. In short, even with weak measures we should have a strong test of whether there is a connection between an accusatory style and self-accusation.

The progressive explanation of inequality makes, of course, a point of being accusatory. Why do blacks have less? Because wealthy whites keep them down. And as a look at figure 3.3 on page 70 will show, the scores of progressives are low on both measures of self-valuation.[5] So on the Personal Competence Index—and the national sample—progressives fall visibly below the average. And on the Self-Esteem Index—and the regional sample—they again fall below the average.

In their broad political outlook and sympathies, progressives are most similar to historicists; in their psychological make-up, however, the two are not all alike. And the difference between them seems to reflect the moralistic, accusatory style of the progressives. This was apparent in their orientations to people, in their readiness to find others untrustworthy; it is apparent also in their orientations toward themselves, in their lack of self-acceptance and self-confidence. In contrast to the progressives, the historicists have positive attitudes toward others and toward themselves.

Individualists fall between the extremes: somewhat lower in self-valuation than historicists, higher than progressives. It is true that some studies of conservatives have found just the reverse: that conservatives lack self-confidence and self-esteem.[6] Doubtless, this holds for some forms of conservatism; not necessarily for all, however. In particular, individualism embraces an integral theme in the popular culture, not some narrow or partisan doctrine. The figure of Horatio Alger summarizes an idea so familiar and so widely shared. And in sharing the ideas of the average American, the individualists show themselves to be average Americans, without an excess of hostility about others or of anxiety about themselves.

+ 1

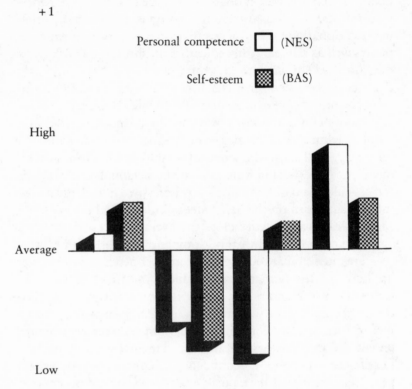

Personal competence ☐ (NES)

Self-esteem ▦ (BAS)

High

Average

Low

− 1

Individualist   Progressive   Fundamentalist   Historicist

FIGURE 3.3
Self-Valuation, Controlling Education

NOTE: On both measures, p is less than .05.

Finally, the evidence on self-valuations of the fundamentalists is mixed. On the Personal Competence Index they are the
lowest scorers. On the Self-Esteem Index, however, they are
slightly above average. It is only prudent, therefore, to resist
a firm conclusion, though our suspicion, if we may voice it,
is fundamentalists do suffer a lack of confidence in themselves.

ATTITUDES TOWARD GOVERNMENT

A generation ago, the ideas defining liberalism seemed settled:
assistance for the jobless, the poor, the elderly, the deprived;
government activism, particularly at the national level; an ex-
tension of the principle of tolerance, understood in political
terms, culminating in the drive for civil liberties and civil rights
for blacks. But in the 1970s the liberal program, so understood,
seemed increasingly to belong to an earlier era in politics when
the opponents of liberalism were conservatives; with the failure
of Johnson's Presidency, the most virulent attack on liberalism
seemed to come from liberals.

The liberal schism that opened in the 1960s took on aspects
of a theological drama of reformation and counterreformation.
Part of the drama centered on whether America represented
a tendency of history that was, on balance, progressive and decent or one that was radically flawed. The desire to disparage
America, particularly to see the war in Vietnam as the outcome, and the proof, of American imperialism, was especially
strong among the militant left. But Vietnam was not the only
source of this sense of Amerika (as some spelled it then) as in-
herently exploitative and indecent. As fundamental was the
problem of racial inequality. For the fact that blacks are manifestly worse off than whites has been for many evidence of the
unreality, even the hypocrisy, of the American dream.

This is, of course, close to the view of the progressives.
The fundamental reason for racial inequality, they feel, is exploitation: The wealthy and powerful rip off the poor and pow-
erless. Victims should not be blamed for being victimized; and
blacks are victims of a society that speaks of equality and practices exploitation.

Hostility to America and its leading institutions—government, industry, multiversity—broke into the open in the 1960s. And liberalism itself seemed to divide, as some liberals denounced America. The question of America—of the extent to which it represents a flawed, even racist, idea—was not the only division among liberals. Shils, for example, speaks of the rise of "collectivist liberalism"; Huntington, of the resurgence of evangelical politics.[7] But most informed observers of American politics agree that a wing of liberalism became estranged in the 1960s. One expression of this was an estrangement from the institutions of politics. And this estrangement, too, the progressives share with the fundamentalists.

We have two measures at hand—one in the NES, one in the BAS—of attitudes toward the institutions of politics. The first is the so-called Trust in Government Index.[8] This is the most widely used of measures of political alienation, a unique barometer of popular confidence in government for a quarter-century. The Trust in Government Index captures the extent to which citizens have a broad faith in the integrity of government. The high scorer feels, characteristically, that the government in Washington can be trusted to do what is right, most of the time at least; that government is run for the benefit of the people; and that government, though it may waste some money, does not really waste a lot of it. In contrast, the low scorer is of the opinion that government is a poor bet to be trusted, that it is pretty much run by a few big interests, and that it is very wasteful.

Attitudes toward government were measured in the BAS study by combining questions on the honesty of government officials, the power of special interests, a sense of belonging and pride in government, and the political influence of the ordinary citizen.[9]

As figure 3.4 shows, progressives tend to see the government as untrustworthy, unresponsive, and unrepresentative; they are below average on the Trust in Government Index in the NES and on the Political Trust Index in the BAS. The attitudes of individualists and historicists to government are rather different. Both are comparatively positive in their attitude toward govern-

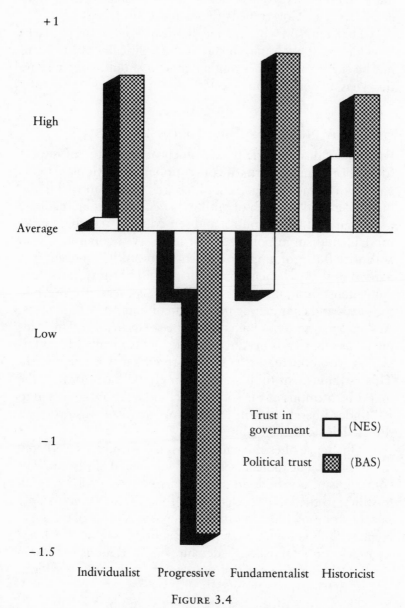

+1

High

Average

Low

−1

−1.5

Trust in
government ☐ (NES)

Political trust ▨ (BAS)

Individualist   Progressive   Fundamentalist   Historicist

FIGURE 3.4
Attitudes toward Government

NOTE: On both measures, *p* is less than .05.

ment; in both surveys, historicists and individualists score higher on Trust in Government than progressives do.

That a person who sees the disadvantaged status of blacks as evidence of exploitation should be politically cynical cannot be surprising; that a fundamentalist should largely share this view is perhaps unexpected, and it deserves comment.

A Note on "Pseudoconservatism"

Fundamentalist rhetoric makes much of the virtue of respect for authority in the form of conventional institutions: parents and family, teachers and school, church and country. Fundamentalism makes much of authority because it is an ideology of restraint, of social control and self-control. Yet what marks fundamentalism in politics is not unreserved commitment to authority but profound ambivalence toward it.[10] Indeed, it is hard to miss the elements of suspicion and hostility in the fundamentalist outlook, beginning with the conservative sweep in the 1920s and culminating in the anticommunism of the 1950s. And of what have fundamentalists been suspicious? The leading ideas and trends in American life—liberalism and secularization—were increasingly seen as threats to Christian faith. This estrangement took an increasingly political form as the major institutions of the society, including schools, seemed to fall under liberal control; Dewey's pragmatism was no less a threat than Roosevelt's liberalism.

This sense of estrangement was, if anything, exacerbated in the 1950s. The radical right, with its yoke of Christian anticommunism, was built around an ideology of suspicion, even hostility, to the larger society. The John Birch Society is only one illustration of how thoroughgoing is this sense of estrangement, with its conspiratorial interpretation of American politics; its attacks on established leadership, on the right as well as on the left, challenging not just their competence but their loyalty and patriotism.[11]

The nature of this estrangement is important to understand, for it helps us to understand a habit of thought familiar to American politics: pseudoconservatism.

Fundamentalism is a form of pseudoconservatism, to use Richard Hofstadter's famous term.[12] Why "pseudo"? Because it involves "a disorder in relation to authority."[13] But how exactly is the pseudoconservative's relation to authority different from the ordinary citizen's? According to studies of authoritarianism, the telltale sign is ambivalence. A disordered orientation to authority manifests itself in an overreadiness simultaneously to defer to the strong, or those higher in status, and to deprecate the weak, or those lower in status.[14] This is the psychology of the bully: Kick those below, bow to those above. And it is the hallmark of the pseudoconservative, according to political historians such as Hofstadter.

For our part, we think that fundamentalists offer a salutary example of how an interpretation, even if right at a psychological level, can be misleading at a political one. For what gives the pseudoconservative away is precisely suspicion and resentment of prevailing trends and leaders: not the unsuccessful or out-of-date or weak but the very opposite: the Trilateral Commission, Earl Warren and the Supreme Court, diplomats in pinstripe suits with bowler hats.

Here, we think, is a key to the politics of the pseudoconservative: Feeling dominated, they resent the dominant. Their resentment and suspicion are directed against the leading tendencies in the culture, the figures and fashions and opinion that are in the ascendancy, at the center of society. Once this is understood, it is not surprising that this estrangement takes the form of pseudoconservatism, not pseudoliberalism. For the dominating political ideas have been liberal. And to the degree that people who feel dominated dislike what is dominant, fundamentalists are moved by the appeal of pseudoconservatism.

Fundamentalists, we are suggesting, take their cues from opinion in the larger society. They may wish to keep clear of it, even to ignore it—but they cannot. Theirs is an oppositional mentality, and theirs is the opposite side to the prevailing side; the mark of their minds is contrariety.

How should this contrariety express itself? Our two samples give us a chance to find out, for the climate of opinion in the nation as a whole and in northern California differed greatly in 1972. An example or two will make the point.[15] Asked what shape the country is in, 34 percent of the BAS sample replied, "something is very wrong," compared to only 18 percent of the NES sample. Well over two-thirds in the national sample thought that the country was in fairly good shape, or even in very good shape; in contrast, less than one-half of the BAS sample was similarly sanguine. A solid majority of the BAS sample went so far as to declare that change in the form of government was necessary; in contrast, an equally solid majority of the NES sample took the opposite point of view.[16] To offer a last example, most citizens in the country as a whole at this time thought that the government could always or most always be trusted to do what is right; in contrast, most citizens in the Bay Area felt it could be trusted only sometimes or never. These data, of course, were gathered in 1972, before the full impact of Watergate was registered. At that time, the Bay Area was, quite simply, far more cynical and alienated than was the country as a whole.

How do fundamentalists score on our measures of political estrangement in the two surveys? The reaction of fundamentalists would seem to depend greatly on the prevailing climate of opinion. As we have seen, in the country as a whole, fundamentalists tend to score low on trust in government; as figure 3.4 shows, in the Bay Area, they tend to score high on political trust.

We take these results to suggest that when government is under attack from the left, fundamentalists will come to its defense and say that public officials can and will do the right thing. Absent heavy attack from the left, fundamentalists will themselves express these very criticisms of a lack of trustworthiness and integrity in government. For disaffection is now the reflexive response of fundamentalists to American society, just as it is the reflex of progressives.

CONCLUSION

There are, then, telling similarities between two attitudes of mind otherwise dissimilar: the fundamentalist and the progressive. The one explains inequality in terms of divine punishment, the other in terms of economic exploitation. Yet there is a close resemblance between them on two points: the stance they take toward themselves and toward society.

The attitude of the fundamentalist and the progressive to self and to society is accusatory and judgmental. This is, we would emphasize, a matter of emphasis, of degree; but it is large enough to make plain the note of misanthropy common to both fundamentalists and progressives. And in this accusatory attitude of mind we can make out themes of moralism common to the two: disapproval, suspicion, and estrangement. This moralistic estrangement from American life provides common ground to those who view racial inequality as God's punishment and those who see it as economic exploitation. In contrast, it is precisely the individualists' identification with the American experience that makes the idea of equality problematic for them, as we see in the next chapter.

NOTES

1. For an extended and instructive account of moral indignation as an affect, see A. F. Davies, *Skills, Outlooks, and Passions* (Cambridge, England: Cambridge University Press, 1980), 318-29.
2. Here we have explicitly followed the procedure of Miller and Levitin. See Warren E. Miller and Teresa E. Levitin, *Leadership and Change: The New Politics and the American Electorate* (Cambridge, Mass.: Winthrop, 1976). For an explanation of our coding and scoring rules, see appendix B.
3. The seminal study documenting this connection between ideology and misanthropy is Herbert McClosky, "Conservatism and Personality," *American Political Science Review* 52 (1958): 27-45.
4. For question wording and scoring rules, see appendix B.
5. Again, these figures reflect differences in self-valuation by explanatory mode *after* controlling the impact of education.
6. See McClosky, "Conservatism and Personality"; for a more recent study, see Glenn D. Wilson, ed., *The Psychology of Conservatism* (New York: Academic Press, 1973).
7. Edward Shils, "The Antinomies of Liberalism," in *The Relevance of Liberalism*, ed. Research Institute on International Change (Boulder, Colo.: Westview Press, 1978); and Samuel P. Huntington, *American Politics: The Promise of Disharmony* (Cambridge, Mass.: Belknap Press, 1981).

8. The three-item version of the Trust in Government Index is being used, following Miller and Levitin, *Leadership and Change*. For an explanation of our coding and scoring rules, see appendix B.
9. For question wording and scoring rules, see appendix B.
10. Marsden traces this thesis of ambivalence in detail in his historical study of fundamentalism. See George M. Marsden, *Fundamentalism and American Culture* (New York: Oxford University Press, 1980).
11. As an example of what we have in mind here, consider the statement of Robert Welch, leader of the John Birch Society: "Treason is widespread and rampant in our high army circles." Quoted in Alan F. Westin, "The John Birch Society," in *The Radical Right*, ed. Daniel Bell (Garden City, N.Y.: Anchor Books, 1964), 245.
12. Richard Hofstadter, *The Paranoid Style in American Politics* (New York: Vintage Books, 1967).
13. Ibid.
14. T. W. Adorno, Else Frenkel-Brunswik, Daniel J. Levinson, and R. Nevitt Sanford, *The Authoritarian Personality* (New York: Norton, 1950).
15. These figures are drawn from Jack Citrin, Herbert McClosky, J. Merrill Shanks, and Paul M. Sniderman, "Personal and Political Sources of Political Alienation," *British Journal of Political Science* 5 (1975): 1-31.
16. The questions varied in wording. In the regional study, the question was put in terms of a need for "a whole new system of government," in the national one for "a big change" only. Then, too, in the regional study the focus was on "our *form* of government," in the national one on "our *system* of government." The likely effect of such wording differences, we suspect, is to have diminished the size of the differences between samples that we should have observed otherwise—differences that were substantial nonetheless.

CHAPTER 4

INDIVIDUALISM

The idea of equality is a hard one to live by for many reasons, but at least one of them is built into the American creed: individualism.

INDIVIDUALISM AND SUPPORT
FOR EQUALITY

There are theoretical reasons to expect a relation between how people account for the fact of inequality and how much they support the value of equality. In particular, some social-psychological theories of giving help suggest that individualists are especially likely to resist efforts to ensure racial equality.[1] From this perspective, whether people tend to give help to a person in difficulty depends on whether they attribute the problem to internal and controllable factors; simply put, if they believe a problem is of a person's own making, they are not inclined to help. So, if they confront someone in a subway who is befuddled and disoriented, they will tend to help if they believe he or she is ill, not to help if they believe he or she is drunk. The individualist account of racial inequality, of course, attributes inequality squarely to internal and controllable factors—that is, to a lack of effort on the part of blacks. And so we should expect the individualist to oppose policies designed to ensure equality.

To assess support for government efforts to realize equal rights for blacks we have taken advantage of two questions:

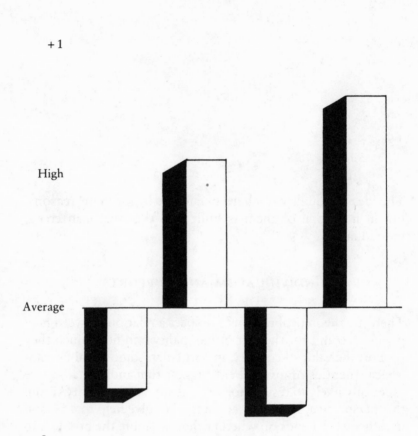

+1

High

Average

Low

−1

Individualist   Progressive   Fundamentalist   Historicist

FIGURE 4.1
Equality as Policy (NES)

NOTE: *p* is less than .05.

1. Should the government in Washington see to it that black people get fair treatment in jobs or leave these matters to the states and local communities?
2. Do you think the government in Washington should see to it that white and black children go to the same schools or stay out of this area as it is not its business?[2]

These two items have been combined to form an additive index —Equality as Policy.

Figure 4.1 shows the relation between explanations of inequality and support for equality as policy. Plainly, historicists and progressives favor equal rights policies. By comparison, individualists score low. So, too, do fundamentalists; a person persuaded that God has consigned blacks to their place is not inclined to be enthusiastic about efforts to improve it.[3]

But perhaps, it can be argued, individualists and fundamentalists do not object to racial equality per se; rather, they object to the federal government's taking on the responsibility of enforcement. After all, a person can oppose a particular policy strategy for realizing racial equality yet sincerely favor racial equality as a value.

To test this conjecture we have built a measure of attitudes toward racial equality as a principle. To support racial equality means to oppose racial discrimination. Accordingly, two items were combined to form an index of Support for Equality in Principle:

1. Which of these two statements would you agree with:
   a. White people have a right to keep black people out of their neighborhoods if they want to.
   b. Black people have a right to live wherever they can afford to, just like anybody else.
2. Are you in favor of desegregation, strict segregation, or something in between?[4]

As we observed in chapter 1, the principle of racial equality now commands general support. This is apparent also in the index we have built. Scores can vary from a low of 2 to

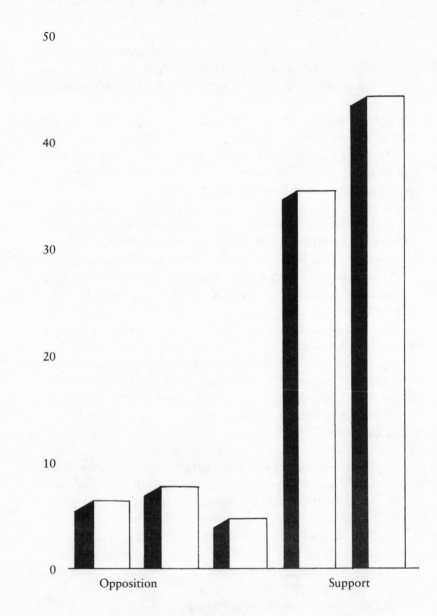

FIGURE 4.2
Support for Equality in Principle (NES) (in percent)

a high of 6. As figure 4.2 shows, the distribution of scores for the index is markedly skewed: Eighty percent of the respondents earn a score of 5 or 6, only 15 percent a score of 2 or 3. This is another way of saying, of course, that most favor the principle of racial equality. But all the same, they do not favor it equally; and so we must look at the relation between type of explanation for the fact of inequality and degree of support for the principle of equality.[5]

The relation between explanation and equality at the level of principle parallels that of explanation and policy, as figure 4.3 on page 86 shows. Again, individualists and fundamentalists score low, historicists and progressives high.

Some caution is required. There is a warehouse of findings showing that support for the value of racial equality and education is strongly and positively related.[6] Since individualists and fundamentalists have had substantially less education than either historicists or progressives, their relative lack of support for equality may reflect only the fact that they have spent less time in schools.

Then, too, a lack of support may have an entirely straightforward cause, independent of the kind of explanation offered for racial inequality, namely, dislike of blacks. Accordingly, we must see how type of explanation and support for the principle of equality are related *after* the effects of education and feeling toward blacks are removed.

As figure 4.4 on page 87 shows, the picture changes. Statistically controlling both education and feelings toward blacks has a significant effect. Historicists and progressives, though still above the average, do not score as high as before. The fundamentalists, moreover, are distinctive no longer; they favor the principle of racial equality as much as the average (white) American, though they plainly favor it less than historicists and progressives.[7] Not so the individualists. Even after both education and feelings toward blacks are eliminated, individualists score below average.

In short, individualists alone resist supporting the value of racial equality at the level of policy and at the level of principle.

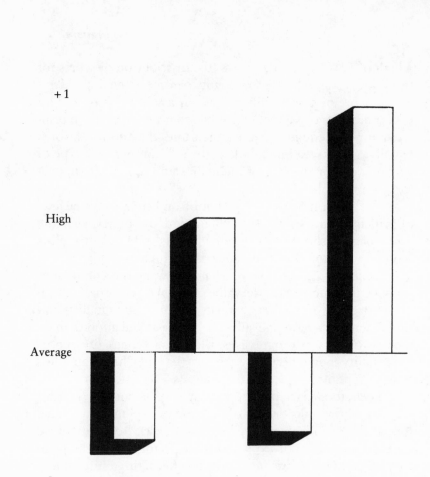

+1

High

Average

Low

−1

Individualist Progressive Fundamentalist Historicist

FIGURE 4.3
Equality in Principle (NES)

NOTE: p is less than .05.

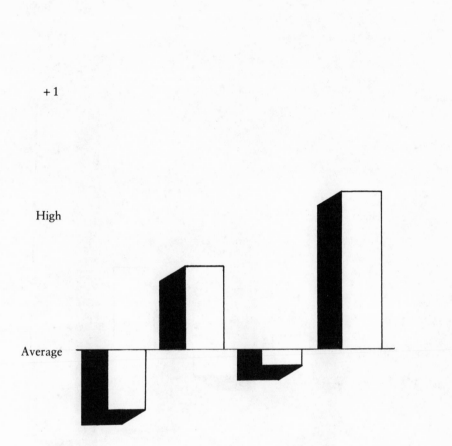

+1

High

Average

Low

−1

Individualist   Progressive   Fundamentalist   Historicist

FIGURE 4.4
Equality in Principle, Controlling Education and Feelings about Blacks (NES)

NOTE: p is less than .05.

+1

High

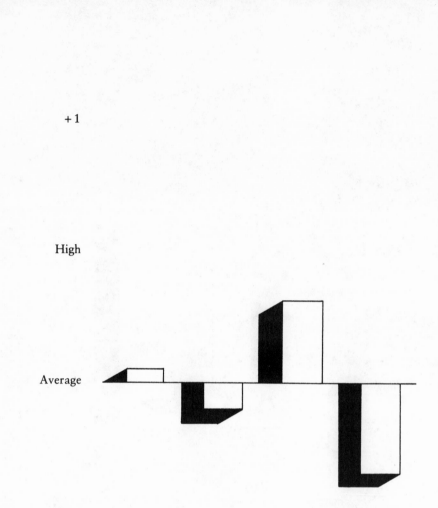

Average

Low

−1

Individualist   Progressive   Fundamentalist   Historicist

FIGURE 4.5
Religiosity, Controlling Education (NES)

NOTE: *p* is less than .05.

PARTICULARISM

Fundamentalism, like individualism, does not encourage support for equality; this is plain at the level of policy, less dramatic (but still significant) at the level of principle. So it is well to try to be clearer about the nature of fundamentalism before turning our attention to individualism. The point to appreciate about fundamentalists is not that they are religious—most Americans are, in some sense or other—but that they are religious in a particular way.

What sets fundamentalism apart may be that it involves religious sentiments that are distinctively punitive and judgmental. But this is only supposition on our part; it is necessary, therefore, to get some sense of the extent to which fundamentalism does in fact represent a religious temper distinctive in degree and, possibly, in kind.

A measure of religiosity was built by putting together two questions:

1. Do you believe that God sends misfortune and illness on people for their sins or not?
2. Do you feel that someone who doesn't believe in God can be a good American?

Scoring high on this Index of Religiosity involves not only being religious but also having a religious outlook of a special kind. It is a religious outlook predicated on exclusivity—on the belief, that is, that other people are less worthy than oneself and that they will suffer divine punishment on this account.[8] Thus the notion that sickness and misfortune are divine punishments for sins provides a proper companion to the idea that racial inequality has divine sanction. The belief that an atheist cannot be a good American also captures this quality of being quick to sit in judgment of others, to view others in a particularistic way, and to be ready to exclude them as outsiders, as sinners.

Figure 4.5 shows the scores of the four explanatory modes on the Religiosity Index.[9] Fundamentalists, not surprisingly, score the highest. Both historicists and progressives score below the average, though it should be observed that the former's aversion to religiosity of this kind is more pronounced than the latter's. But it is the comparison—one is almost tempted to say the contrast—between fundamentalists and individualists that is the most instructive. For the two visibly differ: The former score well above the average; not the latter, however. To all intents and purposes, religiosity is a distinguishing characteristic of the fundamentalist.

This may seem an inevitable result, but a moment's reflection will make plain this is not so. Recall the steps in constructing the inequality typology. First, we identified the individualist and the progressive; only then did we identify the fundamentalist and the historicist. One consequence of proceeding in this two-step fashion was this: A large number of individualists (in fact, 50 percent in the NES and 41 percent in the BAS), in addition to believing that racial inequality is attributable to the "fact" of blacks not trying hard enough, *also* believe—just as the fundamentalist does—that "the differences [between the races] are brought about by God; God made the races different as part of His divine plan."

Even so, individualists and fundamentalists differ markedly in religiosity. And the fact that they do suggests that to have a sense of people's point of view one must find out not only what they believe but also what they do *not* believe. For what distinguishes fundamentalists and individualists are not the factors that they believe are responsible for racial inequality but the ones they believe are *not* responsible. To put the point concretely, what distinguishes fundamentalists is that they accept a divine explanation of inequality, and just as important, they reject a characterlogical one. In a word, not only their beliefs but their disbeliefs matter.

The pattern of beliefs and disbeliefs, we would suggest, gives away the nature of fundamentalist resistance to equal rights. And its basis is the accusatory, punitive strain of moralism. This strain is apparent in the array of beliefs that characterizes the fundamentalist. The notion, for example, that someone who is sick is only getting his or her just deserts is of a piece with the misanthropic notion that people are interested only in what is good for them and will take advantage the first chance they get.

Fundamentalism is moralism on the right. The moralistic resentment and hostility of fundamentalists is at the root of their resistance to equal rights. The resistance arises not because fundamentalists are religious—far and away, most Americans are religious—nor because they are more religious than other Americans are; there is no evidence for this. But the fundamentalist is religious in a specific way: The fundamentalist is particularistic.[10]

The nub of religious particularism is a division of the world into two camps: those who are chosen, who accept and exemplify the true faith, and those who are not, who follow false gods and false paths. Fundamentalists are given to particularism in politics as in religion. This is apparent in their conviction that blacks do not belong, indeed that they have been set aside and condemned to inferiority by God Himself. And from their particularism, with its hostility and lack of sympathy for those who are different and not among the chosen, it is a short step to resist any suggestion that the natural order of racial inequality, ordained by God, should be overturned at the behest of the government in Washington.

INDIVIDUALISM AS A FOLK IDEOLOGY

A belief in individualism also has consequences in and of itself. It is an idea that, once accepted, carries with it a certain view of the world. But what, more concretely, does it signify? What does the individualist understand equality to mean?

A first step in answering these questions is to examine the individualist's understanding of the idea of equal opportunity. To assess this we have put together four questions, each of which asks people to choose between opposing points of view on the extent to which blacks have the same opportunities as whites. They are:

1. *a.* It's a lack of skill and abilities that keep many black people from getting a job. It's not just because

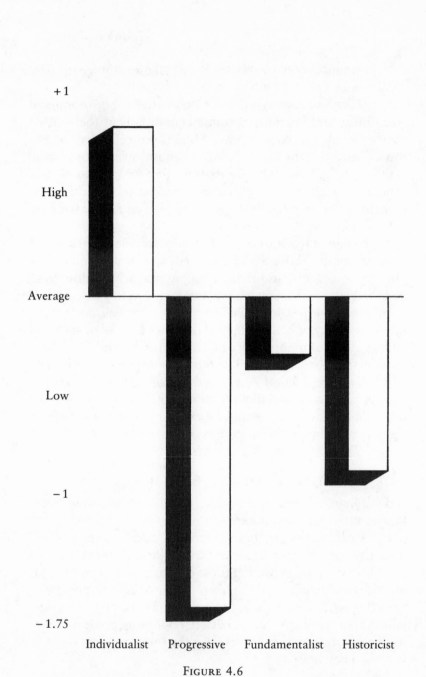

+ 1

High

Average

Low

− 1

− 1.75

Individualist   Progressive   Fundamentalist   Historicist

FIGURE 4.6
Equality of Opportunity for Blacks, Controlling Education (NES)

NOTE: *p* is less than .05.

they're black. When a black person is trained to
do something, he is able to get a job.

   b. Many qualified black people can't get a good job.
White people with the same skills wouldn't have
any trouble.

2.   *a.* Many blacks have only themselves to blame for not
doing better in life. If they tried harder, they'd
do better.

   b. When two qualified people, one black and one
white, are considered for the same job, the black
won't get the job no matter how hard he tries.

3.   *a.* Many black people who don't do well in life do
have good training, but the opportunities just
always go to whites.

   b. Black people may not have the same opportunities as whites, but many blacks haven't prepared
themselves enough to make use of the opportunities that come their way.

4.   *a.* Blacks and other minorities no longer face unfair
unemployment conditions. In fact, they are favored in many training and job programs.

   b. Even with the new programs, minorities still face
the same old job discrimination once the program is over.

These four questions are all different ways of asking one
fundamental question: Do blacks suffer discrimination or, are
they from a lack of training or skills, or indeed, even with the
advantage of special programs, simply not able to make the
most of their opportunities? Figure 4.6 shows the relative standing of individualists on the Opportunity Index. Individualists—
and they alone—score above the average; this is so even after
controlling for education.

There is something extraordinary, we would suggest, about
the individualists' understanding of equality of opportunity.
For it holds, quite simply, that blacks *in fact* are not disadvantaged by virtue of being black. On this view, blacks have not
been victims of discrimination; they have not gotten jobs be-

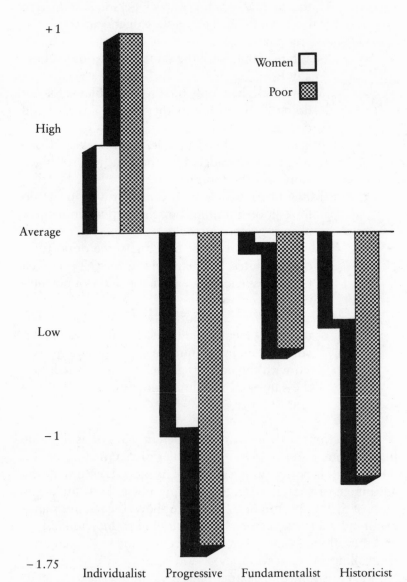

FIGURE 4.7
Equality of Opportunity for Women and the Poor,
Controlling Education (NES)

NOTE: On both measures, *p* is less than .05.

cause they have lacked the qualifications, including a willingness to work hard. And if blacks are qualified, they have the same opportunities as whites.

It would be one thing if individualists took this position only about blacks; in fact, they take it across the board. To show this we have put together measures of Equality of Opportunity for women and for the poor. For the first, people were asked to agree or disagree with these statements:

1. Women have less opportunity than men to get the education for top jobs.
2. Many qualified women can't get good jobs; men with the same skills have much less trouble.
3. Our society discriminates against women.

For the second, people agreed or disagreed with these:

1. With all the training programs and efforts to help the poor, anyone who wants to work can get a job these days.
2. The poor are poor because the American way of life doesn't give all people an equal chance.
3. Poor people didn't have a chance to get a good education — schools in poor neighborhoods are much worse than other schools.

They then chose one of each of these two pairs of items:

4. *a.* People who are born poor have less chance to get ahead than other people.
    b. People who have the ability and work hard have the same chance as anyone else, even if their parents were poor.
5. *a.* Many poor people simply don't want to work hard.
    b. The poor are poor because the American way of life doesn't give all people an equal chance.

The individualists alone scored high on the Index of Equality of Opportunity for Women, as figure 4.7 shows.[11] What sets the individualists apart, then, is the degree to which they reject the suggestion that men have greater opportunities than women or that women, by virtue of being women, have been held back or discriminated against.

The results are even more pronounced in terms of opportunity for the poor. Individualists distinguish themselves by their insistence that being poor is not really a handicap. As the individualist sees it, the poor have the same chance as anyone else; they can get a good education, or a job, if only they want it. Individualism, then, is more than exhortation; it rests on a view of the way the world is, of what the facts are. And the fact, so far as the individualist can make out, is that everyone can get ahead, regardless of whether he or she is black, female, or poor. In a word, to say that individualists believe that everyone has an equal opportunity misses the point; they are so persuaded of this that it is fairer to say that, according to individualists, not only is there equality of opportunity but, more fundamentally, there is equality of condition.

Moreover, individualism is a theory of individual responsibility: it is up to each person to deal with one's problems on one's own, whether they are of one's own making or not. And this suggests another respect in which the individualist view is distinctive: how people should cope with discrimination. The NES included two questions directly on this point:

1.   *a.* Discrimination affects all black people. The only way to handle it is for blacks to organize together and demand rights for all.

           b. Discrimination may affect all blacks but the best way to handle it is for each individual to act like any other American — to work hard, get a good education, and mind his own business.

2.   *a.* The best way for blacks to overcome discrimination is through pressure and social action.

           b. The best way to overcome discrimination is for each individual black to be even better trained and more qualified than the most qualified white person.

They have been combined to form an Index of Black Response to Discrimination. As figure 4.8 on page 98 shows, the individualists score highest;[12] more than anyone else, they believe that blacks can and should overcome discrimination, not through collective organization and group pressure, but by each working harder, getting more schooling and better training; in a word, through individual effort.

In short, individualists believe that blacks have only themselves to blame for not getting ahead; and the same goes for women.[13] And it is up to everyone to deal with his or her special problems on his or her own, without asking for special treatment.

Individualism, then, is an ethic: It is a bedrock belief in an ethic of self-reliance. Individuals must take care of themselves. They must not pretend to be victims of circumstance, or ask for special favors, in an effort to get others to do for them what they should do for themselves. It is up to them to do what it takes to get ahead. They themselves must shoulder the responsibility for their lives; and they must be ready to accept responsibility for their failures, as well as take credit for their successes, instead of patting themselves on the back for the latter while blaming somebody else for the former.

On this view, everyone has to show some character, to stand on his or her own feet. And if people have a chance to make something of themselves, they have only themselves to blame if they fail; and for them to complain, say, about discrimination, is an attempt to duck responsibility for making their own lives work.

Individualism, so conceived, is an ungenerous idea. It is not ungenerous in the sense of being misanthropic. But it refuses to acknowledge that some are in fact handicapped and must overcome obstacles that are not of their making and that others do not face. In this sense the individualists lack empathy for those disadvantaged by race or by poverty or by gender. And this lack of generosity is not an accident of the particular questions we have asked nor a transient effect of the particular historical moment we have studied; it is built into the idea of individualism.

+1

High

Average

Low

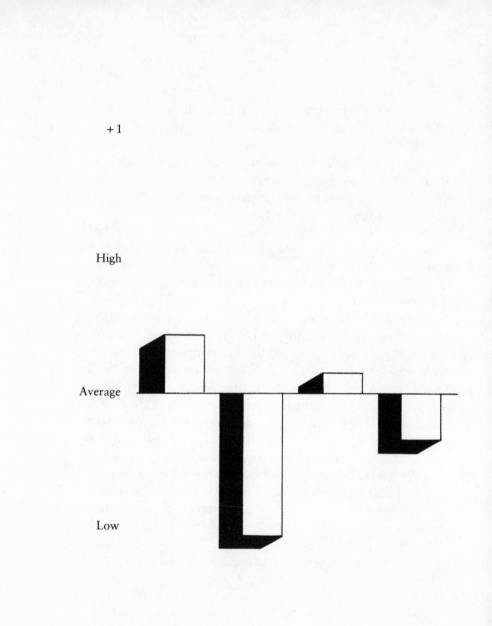

−1

Individualist   Progressive   Fundamentalist   Historicist

FIGURE 4.8
Black Response to Discrimination, Controlling Education (NES)

NOTE: *p* is less than .05.

INDIVIDUALISM AND THE AMERICAN ETHOS

In the American experience individualism has stood for two different things: self-reliance and nonconformity.[14] The first is the individualism of Frederick Jackson Turner; self-reliance is the theme of the frontier, with its premium on hardiness, initiative, physical adaptiveness, and an ability to make do with little and get along without others to fall back upon. The second is the individualism of Alexis de Tocqueville. Not the pioneer, but the dissenter, the nonconformist, the gifted or exceptional or eccentric heads up this version of individualism. Its concern is individuality itself, under a leveling pressure to uniformity, to mediocrity.

Our concern is with the individualism of Turner and not Tocqueville: with the importance that Americans have attached to individual effort, perserverance, independence, and ingenuity. This ethic of self-reliance runs through this country's experience, forming a deep-rooted and distinctively American tradition of thought.

A paradigmatic expression of this tradition, Social Darwinism, an outlook on society and politics summed up in the catchphrase "survival of the fittest," dominated popular and scholarly thinking in the last third of the nineteenth century. Herbert Spencer, though an Englishman, enjoyed a greater vogue in America than in England. Social Darwinism gave a stamp of approval to unrestricted competition.

Darwin had discovered the evolutionary principle: natural selection. Evolution was the unintended outcome of an unremitting struggle for competitive advantage. And as nature was "red in tooth and claw," so also was society. Unfettered competition in the market would weed out the inefficient, the weak, and the unfit.

Not surprisingly, post-civil war plutocrats snapped up this melding of wealth and merit. But Social Darwinism had a much broader and deeper appeal, for it involved, in the phrase of Hofstadter, a kind of "secular piety."[15] The gospel of Charles Darwin, as preached by Herbert Spencer and William Graham Sumner was a gospel of effort, discipline, and struggle. Work was, above all, a way to forge a person's character; achievement was a proof of hard work, responsibility, and self-sufficiency; failure was a punishment for those who were, in Sumner's words, "negligent, shiftless, inefficient, silly and imprudent."[16]

Under the banner of Social Darwinism, individualism showed itself an expression of ascetic Protestantism. It was an ethic of economy, of industry. Competition—unrestricted—was society's means of molding character, enforcing discipline, and preventing the "weakening of personality."[17] Ascetic Protestantism has deep roots, of course, in the American experience. It was not dreamed up out of whole cloth to excuse the riches of robber barons; it reaches back to the Indian summer of New England, in the rising years of the nineteenth century. Its emblematic figure is Ralph Waldo Emerson.

As the central figure of American Transcendentalism, Emerson chose as his text Self-Reliance: with a hard edge. "In horsemenship he is not the good rider who never was thrown, but rather . . . a man will never be a good rider until he is thrown."[18] His call is for the individual to overcome through struggle, to achieve an independence of opinion and institutions, to persevere in his own cause and overcome opposition by tenacity of purpose. And, in attempting this, the individual must rely on himself. "The best lightning-rod for your protection," writes Emerson, borrowing from Thoreau, "is your own spine."[19]

If Emersonian individualism is, on one side, a philosophy of activism, an argument for striving for self-reliance, it is, on the other, a philosophy of quietism, an argument for staying aloof from efforts on others' behalf. "Let a man's social aims," Emerson insists, "be proportioned to his means and power. I do not pity the misery of a man underplaced: that will right itself presently. . . ."[20] Individuals are on their own. "Help must come from their own bosom . . . no man in God's wide earth is either willing or able to help any other man."

Individualism, so conceived, is uncomfortable, even at odds, with political action. The root of the problem is not the complacency that individualism may encourage. This is an aspect of it, but individualism is not necessarily a defense for the status quo—Thoreau's individualism, after all, was the rock of his argument for civil disobedience. Rather, the crux of the problem is individualism's built-in hostility to association, to joint action, which is the very stuff of politics. So Emerson, aware of the need for reform, argued nonetheless:

> The world is awaking to the idea of union. . . . Men will live and communicate, and plough, and reap, and govern, as by added ethereal power, when once they are united. . . . But this union must be inward, and not one of covenants, and is to be reached by a reverse of the method they use. The union is only perfect when all the uniters are isolated. . . . Each man, if he attempts to join himself to others, is on all sides cramped and diminished. . . ."[21]

Uniters isolated, that is radical egoism; and its source: Puritanism. Our concern is not to explore the reasons for a connection between Protestantism and individualism, nor all the forms this connection has taken. Here we wish only to convey something of the intensity of Puritan individualism. An especially vivid illustration of this is salvational imagery. Radical individualism adds a signal horror to the Day of Judgment. As Perry Miller has observed: "The Day of Doom became in effect rugged individualism run riot. . . . The regenerate brother sorrows not a jot over the condemnation of his reprobate twin, the godly sheds no tear over the fate of her erstwhile dear mate, and the adoring husband suddenly ceases to care about the wife who has become 'a damned forsaken wight'; and even

> The tender Mother will own no other of all her numerous brood,
> But such as stand at Christ's right hand acquitted through His blood."[22]

A person need not lack generosity to accept an ungenerous idea; but let him or her hold to it and he or she is in danger of being ungenerous. Individualism's lack of generosity is obscured by misleading images of Horatio Alger and success. They are misleading because applied to inequality, individualism is not a theory of achievement; it is a theory of failure. So it purports to explain why blacks have less than whites, and women have less than men, because they have failed, not because they have been discriminated against. From this perspective, inequality of outcome is not only a consequence of equality of opportunity but a proof of its equity. Americans born black, or women, or the poor, face no special handicaps; they enjoy the same opportunities as everybody else. And if they do not get ahead in life, the responsibility—the fault—is theirs and no one else's. As Emerson asked, "Are they my poor?"

NOTES

1. The most relevant research on this problem has been done by Weiner. See Bernard Weiner, "A Cognitive (Attribution)—Emotion—Action Model of Motivated Behavior: An Analysis of Judgments of Help-Giving," *Journal of Personality and Social Psychology* 29 (1980): 186-200.
2. For this measure, and the one that follows, we are indebted to Mary Jackman. See Mary R. Jackman, "General and Applied Tolerance: Does Education Increase Commitment to Racial Integration?" *American Journal of Political Science* 22 (1978): 302-24; and Mary R. Jackman, "Education and Policy Commitment to Racial Integration," *American Journal of Political Science* 25 (1981): 256-69. Our treatment of missing data, however, departs from hers; for details of this methodological issue, and a discussion of the role of ideology in support for equality, see Paul M. Sniderman, Richard A. Brody, and James H. Kuklinski, "Policy Reasoning and Political Values: The Problem of Racial Equality," *American Journal of Political Science* (1984): 75-94. For our scoring rules, see appendix B.
3. These differences between explanatory types remain even after eliminating the effects of education and feelings about blacks.
4. For scoring rules, see appendix B.
5. Multiple classification analysis is not well suited to the analysis of variates with severely skewed distributions. Accordingly, we have collapsed the distribution on the Index of Equality in Principle.
6. See especially Herbert H. Hyman and Charles R. Wright, *Education's Lasting Influence on Values* (Chicago: University of Chicago Press, 1979), appendix C.
7. We would emphasize that fundamentalists differ markedly from historicists and progressives. The grand mean—the score of the statistically average

American—is a yardstick that makes intuitive sense; however, the statistical analysis is based on a comparison among group means.

8. For a seminal discussion of the social significance of religious particularism, see Charles Y. Glock and Rodney Stark, *Christian Beliefs and Anti-Semitism* (New York: Harper & Row, 1966).
9. The effects of education have been controlled.
10. Glock and Stark, *Christian Beliefs and Anti-Semitism.*
11. These results are with education controlled.
12. These results are with education controlled.
13. Data not shown.
14. Don E. Fehrenbacher, ed., *History and American Society: Essays of David M. Potter* (New York: Oxford University Press, 1973), 256-76.
15. Richard Hofstadter, *Social Darwinism in American Thought* (Boston: Beacon Press, 1955), 10.
16. Quoted in ibid., 11.
17. Ibid., 98.
18. Quoted in Perry Miller, *The American Transcendentalists* (Garden City, N.Y.: Anchor Books, 1957), 303.
19. Quoted in ibid., 296.
20. Quoted in ibid., 297.
21. Yehoshua Arieli, *Individualism and Nationalism in American Ideology* (Baltimore: Penguin, 1964), 278.
22. John Crowell and Stanford J. Searle, eds., *The Responsibility of Mind in a Civilization of Machines: Essays by Perry Miller* (Amherst: University of Massachusetts Press, 1979), 32.

CHAPTER 5

CONCLUSION

Let us first review some of the principal findings and then see what they may, when considered together, suggest more generally about the American creed.

Nearly all Americans acknowledge that blacks have less of "the good things in life" than whites. Asked why blacks have less, 98 percent of white Americans agree with some explanation for it; they accept the question's premise that blacks in fact have less. This acknowledgment is tacit; but the point remains that practically no one challenges the idea that blacks *are,* and not merely *were,* worse off than whites.

And a great many Americans say that they know why. A willingness to offer an explanation of racial inequality—or more exactly, to agree with one offered to them—may signify little in itself. Questions can be answered in the course of an interview out of courtesy or to avoid appearing uninformed or unintelligent. Still, most whites do seem to have some way to explain why, in a society dedicated to equality, blacks are not equal. The explanations they give can be classified in more than one way, but the one that seems to us most instructive organizes particular reasons for racial inequality into four general kinds of explanations: individualist, fundamentalist, progressive, and historicist.

One way to think of explanations of inequality is in terms of traditionalism and modernism. The four modes of explanation seem to fall along such a continuum. An emphasis on character or on God belongs to long-standing or traditional staples of thought, an emphasis on exploitation or on historical causation to modernist ones. From this perspective, the issue of race in America involves a conflict between old attitudes of mind and new.

This perspective fits some of the facts. Individualist and fundamentalist explanations both appeal to Americans who are older, who have had less education, and who are or who think of themselves as conservative—all of which fits an impression that these ways of looking at inequality belong to older, traditional elements of American culture. Conversely, progressive and historicist explanations appeal to Americans who are young, well educated, and politically liberal—all of which suggests that these two ways of explaining inequality are modernist in character.

But underlying this cleavage in ideas between traditional and modern, and independent of it, is an integral element in the American ethos: moralism. A moralistic strain runs through American politics, its ostensibly pragmatic style notwithstanding. "Americans are eminently prophets," Santayana wrote. "They apply morals to public affairs; they are impatient and enthusiastic. . . . They are men of principles and fond of stating them."[1]

The impress of moralism shows itself in the similarity between the fundamentalist and the progressive in telling ways. That these two should in any way be alike is remarkable, for they are, of course, in many ways polar opposites: One of them sees blacks as victims, the other as sinners. One is on the political left, the other on the right. Yet the two share a common animus. This is apparent in their orientation toward other people in general.

A telling aspect of a person's personal makeup is the extent to which he or she has faith in other people—in the degree to which he or she feels that people are trustworthy, helpful, and fair. Moralism is an accusatory style. It reduces wrong to wrongdoing, a frame of mind fitting one who has little confidence in his fellow citizen, who sees others as undependable, selfish, and unfair. Fundamentalists have little faith in people; so, too, the progressives. The moralism of both is given away by the misanthropy of both.

Conclusion

Moralism shows itself in a second way: in attitudes toward authority. It is not easy in America for moralists to identify with established institutions. This is plain in the case of moralism on the left; the person who thinks that the root of racial inequality is white exploitation is not apt to think that the political process is representative or fair. But neither are moralists on the right. They, too, find it hard to identify with established institutions; for in America, the leading tendencies at the center of politics and culture have been, for more than half a century, liberal and secular. Not surprisingly, the moralistic right feels estranged from the political process, except when it comes under attack from the moralistic left. Otherwise, fundamentalists and progressives alike tend to cynicism, to political alienation.

Moralism is one major theme that emerges as Americans try to account for inequality. A second theme is individualism.

Individualism strikes us as a folk ideology in two senses. First, it is a point of view that predominates in every major part or stratum of society. So it is the most popular explanation for inequality within the working class as well as among the middle class; indeed, it is even more popular among the former than among the latter.

Second, and more important, individualism involves a whole family of ideas. At its center is a way of thinking about achievement, and so about individual responsibility and entitlement. Its emphasis on individual effort—for us its hallmark—is a clue to the idea of causality that underlies it. The individualist says that the reason blacks have less is because they try less, that is, the cause of racial inequality resides within every black individual and is under his or her control.[2]

The nub of individualism, then, is voluntarism: Whether or not people succeed is up to them. This voluntarism finds expression in a number of ways. So individualists distinguish themselves by rejecting suggestions that blacks are handicapped by external factors, such as a lack of training or discriminatory hiring practices. Then, too, individualists are uniquely committed to self-help. They, and they alone, consistently reject the idea that the way to overcome discrimination is through group

109

action, arguing instead that it is up to each person to deal with it on his or her own.

This attitude of mind lies behind the resistance of the individualists to equal rights policy. Their voluntarism, it is worth emphasizing, is causal, not philosophic. They do not resist the federal government's attempts to assure equal rights for blacks from a commitment to a conservative philosophy of states' rights; their objection is independent of liberalism/conservatism, rooted not in abstractions of philosophy but in an understanding of everyday experience. Believe that people can get ahead if only they work at it, and you will be tempted to believe that if they have failed to get ahead, it is precisely because they have failed to work at it. And on this view, having failed to try their hardest, they try to shift the blame, arguing that they never really had a chance, that they are victims of discrimination. But there *is* equal opportunity, the individualist insists; and for blacks to say otherwise amounts to an effort on their part to excuse their failure, to deny their own responsibility for how their lives have turned out.

Finally, their voluntarism makes clear what individualists mean when they say there is equal opportunity. In their view, being born black or female or poor is not a handicap in getting a job and getting ahead. They reject, that is to say, the argument that people's circumstances determine their prospects, believing instead that whether or not people succeed is up to them. In a word, individualists believe not only in equality of opportunity but also in equality of condition.

A QUESTION OF RACISM?

Should this resistance to enforcing equal rights be understood to result from a commitment to an attitude of mind of which many Americans are proud — self-reliance — or one of which they should be ashamed — racism?

There is now a substantial body of research on "symbolic racism."[3] It claims to show that a range of popular policy positions — support for cutting the amount of property tax on homes, for example, or opposition to court-ordered busing —

spring in large part from the racism of American institutions and history, a racism that large numbers of Americans are taught as children or young adults and that often guides their responses to political issues in later years. Is it not possible that many Americans who say that the federal government should not ensure that blacks have equal rights say this because they do not really want blacks to be equal? Or, more fundamentally, is it not possible that the individualist explanation for racial inequality—blacks do not try as hard as whites—is itself an expression of racism?

Symbolic racism, as a term for scholarship, is a witches' brew.[4] As opposed to old-fashioned bigotry, symbolic racism is said to consist of "a conjunction of two separate underlying dimensions: a specifically anti-black attitude, and conservative value priorities, which stress individual effort and responsibility rather than government activism."[5] Is this a fair description of the individualist? Is individualism, at bottom, a form of racism?

Parts of the description would seem to fit well; others, more loosely. Thus it is plainly true that individualists are the most likely to oppose government efforts to help blacks and other minorities and, what is more, that they base their opposition expressly on the ground that it is the responsibility of blacks to deal with their problems themselves. Then, too, individualists do feel slightly less warmly toward blacks than do historicists and progressives.[6]

Yet, one must ask whether it is, on balance, more fair to attribute the individualists' opposition to enforcing equal rights for blacks to their commitment to the ethic of self-reliance or, alternatively, to antiblack feeling on their part? Accepting that these two elements can be mixed together in the minds of some, we think it fits the evidence better to take the individualists at their word—to believe that they are sincere in thinking that success and failure rest in every person's own hands—rather than to suppose that they talk of individual initiative and perseverance so as to camouflage their racism. And the reason to suppose that individualists are sincere is the fact that they judge everyone in the same terms. They do not talk about the importance of individual responsibility and self-help only when they are talking about blacks; they take exactly the same line when it comes to discrimination against women, insisting that women (like blacks) have to deal with it individually, on the job, not collectively, in the courts. Nor do individualists talk about equality of opportunity only when they are asked if blacks do not have a fair chance to get ahead. They insist that any woman (like any black) can get ahead and that being born poor (like being born black) is not a handicap.

In short, individualists are committed to a master idea: Everyone can make it provided only that he or she is willing to try. Individualists do not say they believe this in order to disguise an aversion to blacks that they feel on other grounds; they believe it, and they say so whether they are talking about blacks or women or, for that matter, the poor. They are radical egalitarians.

POPULAR CULTURE AND DEMOCRATIC THEORY

Resistance to enforcing equal rights, then, reflects a belief in the notion of individual responsibility, not prejudice pure and simple. If so, what does this signify about the American ethos and the politics of race? Or, to ask a broader question, what is the relation between popular culture and democratic values?

Democratic values, it is sometimes thought, lack popular support. Not so. Nearly everyone favors them, in the abstract. This is most obviously true of opinion on freedom of speech and thought. There is strong evidence of public backing for citizens' rights to have a chance to talk and be heard; to have the same legal rights and protection as anyone else, whatever their political beliefs; to worship in the church of their choice or, indeed, not to worship at all; to read what they wish, without someone telling them what they may read and what they may not.[7] What is more, there is now general support for once-controversial values like racial equality. As we have seen, a public consensus has formed in favor of the principle of racial equality; open housing, school integration, and equal opportunity in employment, once favored by small minorities, now are approved by overwhelming majorities.

But what, one must ask, does this support for democratic principles actually signify? Even when it is sincere, and sometimes it manifestly is not, to what extent does it reflect a genuine understanding of the ideas and issues involved? On the one side, democratic values are easy to approve, but hard to apply; they are complex and collide with one another and change with time and circumstance. On the other side, citizens know little of politics or political ideas. As we saw in chapter 1, there is strong evidence for a minimalist model of public opinion, particularly on the issue of the depth of public understanding of political ideas and the political process. Large numbers of citizens are unfamiliar with basic ideas of political discourse, such as liberalism/conservatism; they are unaware of basic facts of American politics, such as when their representatives are up for reelection; indeed, they are without any opinion whatever on major issues of public policy such as Medicare or foreign aid. And if they know little about elementary aspects of politics, how much can they be expected to know about genuinely complex matters, such as democratic values?

On this view, democratic values enjoy a layer of support. This layer, however, is thin and chiefly consists of the politically sophisticated and active. In contrast, the average citizen has only a weak grasp of democratic values; the more so, the more politically unsophisticated and apathetic he or she tends to be. In this view of popular culture, the metaphor of high and low, primitive and complex, is controlling. The values of the political culture, properly conceived, are abstract and complex; those of the public at large are oversimplified, archaic. This thesis has been succinctly presented by Gertrude Selznick and Stephen Steinberg:

> For analytic purposes, we can distinguish in the United States between the official, or ideal culture and the unofficial, or common culture. The official culture contains the ideal norms that characterize our society in its public and secular spheres. These norms are derived from scientific and democratic values and represent the cognitive and moral commitments of a society whose political order is

a democracy and whose economy is based on technology. Scientific and democratic values provide ample grounds for rejecting prejudice and discrimination. Intellectually and morally, the official culture is enlightened and unprejudiced.

Alongside the official culture is an unofficial or common culture which not only differs from the ideal culture but is at odds with it. Historically more archaic, the common culture is not only prescientific and predemocratic but antiscientific and antidemocratic. Nevertheless, it is the culture that is normally taken on by Americans unless they acquire criteria for rejecting it.[8]

This view we may call a social learning theory of democratic values. The built-in obstacles to popular understanding of democratic values—the abstractness of these values, their complexity, and above all, the complications of their interconnections—are, on a social learning approach, responsible for the peculiar "two-tiered" structure of political culture. One tier consists of the few, committed to the master values of politics; the other, of the many, with their imperfect understanding of them. The lower tier offers a shadowy reflection of the upper, for the values of the few, mirrored in the minds of the many, tend to be oversimplified, vulgarized—so much so that their very spirit is sometimes misunderstood.

On this view the public at large fails to hold democratic values for much the same reason that fourth-century Christians failed to hold to monotheism—a curious conjunction at first glance; less so on reflection. For, according to David Hume, monotheism is abstract and complex and thus difficult to learn. The privileged few have had the instruction and enjoy the sanctuary required to understand monotheism; in contrast, the many lack intellectual sophistication, and lacking an ability to see through particulars to underlying principles, they see the parts but not the whole. Accordingly, they oversimplify, and under the pressure of fear and hope, personify experience.

As Peter Brown, summarizing Hume's analysis, has written:

"The vulgar . . . being ignorant and uninstructed" tended
to fragment those experiences of abstract order on which
any coherent view of the universe could be based. For the
average man was both notoriously ill-equipped through
lack of instruction to abstract general principles from his
immediate environment; and, in any case, in all but the
most privileged ages, and among the most sheltered elites,
the natural inability of the uninstructed intellect to think
in abstract terms was heightened by fears and anxieties,
which led men to personalize yet further the working of
causes beyond their control, and so to slip deeper into poly-
theistic ways of thought.[9]

Hume's analysis, then, nicely parallels modern democratic
theory. For both, popular culture tends to irrationality and fa-
naticism, to oversimplifying and thus corrupting the values of
the official culture. For both, the repository of these values tends
to be the privileged few, with the education and leisure to take
a firm grip on them. And for both, the views of the many tend
to a repudiation of the official values (to polytheism in the case
of religion, to antidemocratic ideas in the case of politics) because the many lack the intellectual and cultural resources to
understand these necessarily abstract and complex values.

How well does this analysis apply to attitudes toward racial
inequality? It is true that the sources of resistance to assuring
racial equality are fundamentalism and individualism, attitudes
of mind that reflect a simple, perhaps overly simple, view of
the importance of individual qualities relative to economic and
historical factors. And it is true as well that both fundamentalism and individualism have their strongest appeal among the
poorly educated.

Yet there are at least two reasons to suspect that a social
learning explanation, however helpful elsewhere, is not entirely adequate here. First, though many aspects of equal rights
policy are complex and difficult to understand, the rights about
which we inquired seem straightforward, even elemental. There
is nothing abstruse about whether or not blacks should be able
to live wherever they can afford to. In this political culture, at

this time, the answer clearly is that blacks *should* be able to do so; and indeed, we have seen that far and away, most whites have learned this. Second, the individualist and the fundamentalist score low on, for example, the Equality as Policy Index *after* the impact of education is eliminated. Their resistance to equal rights policy springs from their points of view; it does not simply reflect their lack of sophistication or other cognitive ills brought on by a lack of schooling.

A social learning account has much to contribute to an understanding of democratic values. Nonetheless, it is incomplete. For it amounts, at bottom, to an explanation of what people do not believe, not of what they do believe. Why, it asks, are many people not racially tolerant? Because they have failed to learn the value of tolerance as laid out in the official culture. On this view, people come to their view of the world by default. They understand only poorly what they are supposed to believe — the values of the official culture — and to this extent find it hard to see that ideas at odds with these values should be rejected.

Popular culture, then, is what people wind up believing because they do not know any better. But surely a two-tiered theory exaggerates. Popular culture is not simply a poor-quality copy of the official culture; rather, it embodies definite and agreed-upon ideas of right and wrong, ideas coherent on their own terms and passed on from one generation to the next. Popular culture consists in ideas that are well and widely learned; it is not simply a hodgepodge resulting from failure to learn the ideas of the official culture.

Accordingly, much of the popular resistance to equal rights for blacks, far from springing from an unfortunate failure to learn the values of this culture, follows precisely from a commitment to certain of these values. One of these is individualism; another of them, more arguably, is religiosity of a fundamentalist variety. Some popular opposition to equal rights for blacks does reflect a failure to grasp democratic values and to see their relevance to issues like open housing laws. But opposition arises, not only from ignorance or from an erroneous sense of what the values of the American culture are, but also from the breadth of popular commitment to some of the core values themselves, and of individualism preeminently.

Individualism taps a deep strain of the popular culture. The idea of voluntarism is fundamental to American thought, particularly if by American thought we mean the thought of the average American. The notion that anybody can make it, whatever his or her circumstances, if only he or she tries, is a radical idea; it is the foundation for a whole family of ideas that helps establish what people are responsible for and what, therefore, they are entitled to. Fundamentalism, too, represents a deep strain of the popular culture. It reflects the importance not of religion as a category of political thought but of a frankly punitive and judgmental habit of mind, a readiness to divide the world into sinners and saved, together with an unwillingness to trust others—a tendency, that is, to feel hostile or at least suspicious and critical of people.

Both individualism and fundamentalism are at odds with the value of racial equality. But the importance of individualism in particular is not limited to shaping people's sense of the way the world should be; at least as important is its impact on people's sense of the way the world is. So the individualists systematically tend to deny or minimize the problem of inequality. Blacks, they say, do not suffer discrimination; nor are women held back; nor is being born poor a handicap. In short, believing in equality of condition, individualists are radical egalitarians.

Individualism, and to a lesser extent, fundamentalism, help make up the popular culture. There are competing tendencies of thought; witness the historicist and progressive.[10] But individualism dominates the popular understanding of equality and responsibility, with ironic consequence. One source of resistance to racial equality is the very commitment of many Americans to equality.

NOTES

1. Quoted in Samuel P. Huntington, *American Politics: The Promise of Disharmony* (Cambridge, Mass.: Belknap Press, 1981), 67.
2. Causal attributions may be organized on two dimensions: internal/external and controllable/uncontrollable. For a formal analysis of causal attributions in this framework, see Bernard Weiner, "A Cognitive (Attribution)—Emotion—Action Model of Motivated Behavior: An Analysis of Judgments of Help-Giving," *Journal of Personality and Social Psychology* 29 (1980): 186-200.
3. See, for example, David O. Sears and Donald R. Kinder, "Racial Tensions and Voting in Los Angeles," in *Los Angeles: Viability and Prospects for Metropolitan Leadership,* ed. Werner Z. Hirsch (New York: Praeger, 1971); David O. Sears, Carl P. Hensler, and Leslie K. Speer, "Whites' Opposition to 'Busing': Self-Interest or Symbolic Politics?" *American Political Science Review* 73 (1979): 369-84; David O. Sears, Richard R. Lau, Tom R. Tyler, and Harris M. Allen, Jr., "Self-Interest vs. Symbolic Politics in Policy Attitudes and Presidential Voting," *American Political Science Review* 74 (1980): 670-84; and David O. Sears and Jack Citrin, *Tax Revolt* (Cambridge, Mass.: Harvard University Press, 1982).
4. For an extended discussion of the conceptual and methodological failings of research on symbolic racism, see Paul M. Sniderman and Philip E. Tetlock, "Symbolic Racism: Problems of Political Motive Attribution," *Journal of Social Issues,* in press.
5. Sears and Citrin, *Tax Revolt,* 168.
6. Measured by the NES "feeling thermometer."
7. See Herbert McClosky, "Consensus and Ideology in American Politics," *American Political Science Review* 58 (1964): 366.
8. Gertrude J. Selznick and Stephen Steinberg, *The Tenacity of Prejudice* (New York: Harper & Row, 1969), 157. In view of the criticism that we shall be making, it is only fair to observe that it is ourselves, among others, whom we are criticizing. See Paul M. Sniderman, *Personality and Democratic Politics* (Berkeley: University of California Press, 1975).
9. Peter Brown, *The Cult of the Saints* (Chicago: University of Chicago Press, 1981), 14.
10. Here we have focused on the tension between democratic values and the popular culture. But that culture can not only sustain but can excite democratic politics. A task of future research might well be to consider how substantial this speculation is, perhaps by focusing on popular ideas of liberty, as opposed to equality.

TEACHING

It is an unhappy event when teaching and research are divorced. Their separation may be less unhappy in disciplines not lending themselves to collaborative work—literature, for example; however, it is especially to be regretted in the case of quantitative analysis of the kind we have presented here. But preaching sermons on the benefits of a union of teaching and research does little good. Accordingly, we have prepared this appendix to explain how instructors can obtain the data used in our analysis and to suggest specific exercises they and their students can undertake. The quantitative exercises are straightforward, assuming only minimum competence in data processing and statistical analysis. Both quantitative and qualitative exercises are designed to illustrate how the argument of this book can be challenged and extended in the classroom. They also make plain how the presentation of results signals not the end, but the beginning of inquiry.[1]

Before outlining these exercises, we should like to say a word about the data themselves and how to obtain them. The sampling design of the 1972 National Election Study is a familiar one, at least in general terms, and documentation is easily available through the Inter-University Consortium for Political and Social Research. The case is otherwise for the 1972 Bay Area Survey, and though documentation is available on request, we should like to describe briefly the study design.

The sample is a full-probability cluster sample of the five-county San Francisco-Oakland Bay Area. This Standard Metropolitan Statistical Area (SMSA), comprising a total population of 3,109,519 in 1970, takes in five counties: Marin to the north, San Mateo to the south, San Francisco to the west, and Contra Costa and Alameda to the east. The survey was designed and carried out by the continuing field staff of the Survey Research Center at the University of California at Berkeley. The interviewing staff is predominantly professional, although for this study a few were graduate students. All interviewers took part in a two-day training session on the procedures and content of this specific study. The Bay Area Survey employs a three-stage, area-probability sample utilizing the maps and statistical reports of the 1970 U.S. Census as its basic sampling frame. A special black "overlay" was added, for a prejudice study. As our study focuses on nonblacks, the unweighted sample was used ($N = 963$). Interview completion rate (for the regular sampling frame) was 75.4 percent; with respect to noncompleted interviews, 14.6 percent represented direct refusals, 4.0 percent indirect refusals (e.g., broken appointments), and 6.0 percent inaccessible (never at home, ill, out of town, etc.).[2]

Both the NES and BAS studies are available through the Inter-University Consortium for Political and Social Research. Each university belonging to the ICPSR has a consortium representative on campus. Data sets may be ordered through the representative. Alternatively, a letter requesting data sets may be sent to:

Member Services
ICPSR
P.O. Box 1248
Ann Arbor, Michigan 48106

There is, of course, no charge for consortium members (apart from providing a magnetic tape); for nonmembers, estimates of costs will be provided on request.

EXERCISE 1:
POLICY ADVOCACY AND COUNTERADVOCACY
Have students collect newspaper and magazine articles dealing

with a specific public policy. Students are to read carefully the material and then to analyze it in the following manner:

1. What are the advertised goals of this policy?
2. What are the means by which the policy proposes to achieve its goals?
3. What is the connection, if any, between the goals and means of policy, or objections to them, and deep-seated attitudes of mind of the kind we have analyzed?

Example: Some object to birth control clinics providing teenagers with birth control information and contraceptives without the knowledge or consent of their parents. Accordingly they favor a requirement, as a matter of public policy, that clinics receiving money from the federal government notify parents if their children are being treated.

Among the questions one may ask: What is the relation between the goal of preserving traditonal institutions — the family, in this case — and political conservatism? Is there an incongruity about policies that aim to preserve traditional values by means of a federal requirement, or is this only an apparent paradox? How do the conceptions of individual responsibility assumed by advocates of this policy and counteradvocates differ? In grappling with such questions, it can be useful to ask questions about the questions themselves.

Perhaps the key "meta-question" to ask is this: With respect to a specific policy issue, is a minimalist or maximalist model of public opinion (discussed in chapter 1) the more likely to hold? This is a key question to ask because its answer is likely to determine the range of answers to so many other questions.

For example, depending on which of the models holds, one can make an educated guess about (1) how many citizens are likely to be aware, even in broad terms, of the issue; (2) whether their preferences on this policy question are likely to be predictable, given knowledge of their general political outlook; and (3) the size of the potential public constiutency for the policy, were it to become salient.

EXERCISE 2:
ARE IDEAS ABOUT INEQUALITY GENERAL
OR SPECIFIC?

Our analysis has focused on ideas about racial inequality, about the ways in which white Americans explain why blacks have less of the good things than whites. But do Americans, it is natural to ask, account for other *kinds* of inequality in the same way that they account for racial inequality? It is possible to get a rough answer to this question by doing a simple cross-tabulation, using the BAS data.

There are, of course, many kinds of inequality. But with the possible exception of race, it is surely inequality of wealth that most interests students of society and politics. Fortunately, in the BAS a series of questions explore ideas about the reasons why even though America is wealthy, some people are poor. Specifically, the question is:

> As you know, even though America is a wealthy nation, there are still many people living here who are poor. I will read you some reasons people have offered to explain why this is so, and I'd like you to tell me for each whether you agree strongly, agree somewhat, disagree somewhat, or disagree strongly.

Respondents are then handed a card, with six "explanations" of poverty printed on it:

1. The poor are poor because the wealthy and powerful keep them poor.
2. There are poor people because God made it so.
3. Poor people simply don't want to work hard.
4. Being poor is the result of having been born without the talents to get ahead.
5. The poor are poor because the American way of life doesn't give all people an equal chance.
6. Poor people are used to being poor because they grew up with it and it is a way of life for them.

This series of questions about poverty parallels the series about race, though the wording of comparable questions, it is important to note, may not in fact be comparable—certainly it is far from identical. Still, a typology of modes of accounting for economic inequality similar to that of explaining racial inequality can be developed. Operationally, this would mean proceeding in four steps, classifying together:

a. Those agreeing with proposition 1 and disagreeing with proposition 3.
b. Those disagreeing with proposition 1 and agreeing with proposition 3.
c. Those agreeing with proposition 2, who have not been classified yet.
d. Those agreeing with proposition 6, who have not been classified yet.

This procedure, then, yields four groups:[3] *(a)* represents a progressive approach; *(b)* represents an individualist; *(c)* a fundamentalist; and *(d)* a historicist. By cross-tabulating the two typologies it can be seen whether people who explain racial inequality in one way also explain economic inequality in the same way. Thus, one can learn what proportion of those accounting for blacks having less in terms of individualism, for example, explain the problem of economic inequality in similar terms.

Interpreting the relation between the two typologies can be an engaging exercise. For some parts of the question whether Americans think about different kinds of inequality in the same or different ways are obvious, others less so and in need of being teased out. For example, a major point of difference in the ways that Americans think about economic and racial inequality stands out. It concerns the fundamentalist mode of explanation. A substantial number find it perfectly sensible to say that racial inequality has divine sanction; far fewer think that it makes sense to say the same about poverty.

Should this be taken to mean that different kinds of inequality are indeed thought about in different ways—that the ways Americans try to explain racial inequality have no bearing on the ways they try to explain poverty? Looked at from a very narrow angle, the answer may appear to be yes. But it would be worthwhile to consider whether the various explanations "mean" the same thing when applied to different kinds of inequality. Their meaning may be said to be the same, or very similar, to the extent that their causes or consequences are the same or very similar. The task, then, is to compare the correlates of explanations for racial and for economic inequality. It will be helpful to sort these correlates into groups: one approach, of course, being to duplicate the organization of our analysis, chapter by chapter. If done, this may help make clear whether Americans really do have definite ways of thinking, not about this or that form of inequality, but about inequality in general.

Exercise 3:
The Bay Area—Similar or Different?

The Bay Area is obviously different from the country as a whole. One point of difference is the popularity of alternative explanations for racial inequality. As figure 2.2 showed, individualism is substantially more popular nationwide than in the Bay Area, while a progressive approach is markedly more common there than in the country as a whole. What is the reason, it is natural to ask, for this difference?

One way to answer this question is to fix on one or more ways in which the climate of opinion in the Bay Area differs from that of the country as a whole, and account for the difference in ideas about equality as an offshoot of more profound differences in political ethos. An alternative tack, and as it seems to us a preferable one, to be tried first, is simpler and more concrete. It focuses on the fact that in the Bay Area are found more (or fewer) people than in the country generally who have some particular characteristic already demonstrated to be connected with ideas about equality. If so, the appearance of distinctiveness about the Bay Area, though correct descriptively, may be misleading causally. For the operative factor is a difference in the distributions of individuals, not any difference attributable to the Bay Area per se.

What sorts of individual characteristics do we have in mind? Two immediately suggest themselves: education and ideology. People who live in the Bay Area have had, on average, more schooling than people in the country generally; they are also more liberal, certainly in terms of their general outlook and, very likely, in terms of their preferences on a range of specific issues. (The extent of these differences, of course, can be gauged by comparing the frequencies—or "marginals"—reported in the codebook for each study.)

But which of the two, education or ideology, should be considered first? The question has no certain answer, but education would seem the better choice, if only because what a person believes politically may well be a function of how much schooling he or she has had, but how long a person has spent in school is unlikely (freakish cases aside) to be a function of his or her ideology.

This is a formal consideration, but there is a substantive one as well. We have been impressed by the success of hypotheses framed around education. They are conceptually simple, yet often empirically powerful. And not only does education help greatly in accounting for what Americans think about politics; it also helps in accounting for what they do, as Wolfinger and Rosenstone have demonstrated in their classic study of turnout.[4]

It is only one step, then, to see if the popularity of the various explanations for inequality is more nearly the same in the Bay Area as in the nation if we make sure to compare people who have had the same amount of education or who are similarly liberal or conservative. It is necessary, in a word, to run a three-way table, that is, a cross-tabulation illustrating the covariation of two variables, controlling for a third.[5]

NOTES

1. For help in generating exercises we are indebted to Henry Brady and Charles McGuire.
2. For a technical account of the Bay Area Survey, see *Bay Area Survey 2, Study Codebook* (Berkeley: Survey Research Center, University of California, 1975).
3. It is necessary to purge those without any definite opinion on the reasons for poverty, as indicated by their willingness to agree with any explanation for it whatever. See chapter 2.
4. Raymond E. Wolfinger and Steven J. Rosenstone, *Who Votes?* (New Haven: Yale University Press, 1980).
5. For the best account of the logic of tabular analysis, see Morris Rosenberg, *The Logic of Survey Analysis* (New York: Basic Books, 1968).

MEASURES

ISSUE PREFERENCES AND IDEOLOGY

The NES measures of issues preferences and ideology were as follows:

1. Some people feel that the government in Washington should see to it that every person has a job and a good standard of living. Others think the government should just let each person get ahead on his own. And, of course, other people have opinions somewhere in between. Suppose people who believe that the government should see to it that every person has a job and a good standard of living are at one end of this scale — at point number 1. And suppose that the people who believe that the government should let each person get ahead on his own are at the other end — at point number 7. *(Interviewer hands card to respondent.)* Where would you place yourself on this scale, or haven't you thought much about this?

2. Some people are primarily concerned with doing everything possible to protect the legal rights of those accused of committing crimes. Others feel that it is more important to stop criminal activity even at the risk of reducing the rights of the accused. *(Interviewer hands card to respondent.)* Where would you place yourself on this scale, or haven't you thought much about this?

3. Some people feel that the government in Washington should make every possible effort to improve the social and economic position of blacks and other minority groups. Others feel that the government should not make any special effort to help minorities because they should help themselves. *(Interviewer hands card to respondent.)* Where would you place yourself on this scale, or haven't you thought much about this?
4. There is much discussion about the best way to deal with the problem of urban unrest and rioting. Some say it is more important to use all available force to maintain law and order—no matter what results. Others say it is more important to correct the problems of poverty and unemployment that give rise to the disturbances. *(Interviewer hands card to respondent.)* Where would you place yourself on this scale, or haven't you thought much about this?
5. We hear a lot of talk these days about liberals and conservatives. I'm going to show you a seven-point scale on which the political views that people might hold are arranged from extremely liberal to extremely conservative. *(Interviewer hands card to respondent.)* Where would you place yourself on this scale, or haven't you thought much about this?

ANTI-INTELLECTUALISM

The measure of anti-intellectualism was constructed from two items with which respondents were asked to agree or disagree in the NES survey:

1. I prefer the practical man anytime to the man of ideas.
2. People ought to pay more attention to new ideas, even if they seem to go against the American way of life.

On the first item, respondents scored 3 for agreement, 1 for disagreement, 2 for "don't know" or if a response was not available. On the second, the scoring was 3 for disagreement, 1 for agreement, and 2 for "don't know" or if not available. Scores on the two items were added to produce a measure on which 6 represented a high level of anti-intellectualism and 2 a low level of anti-intellectualism.

TRUST IN PEOPLE

The measure of trust in people was constructed from three items in the NES survey:

1. Generally speaking, would you say that most people can be trusted, or that you can't be too careful in dealing with people?
2. Would you say that most of the time people try to be helpful, or that they are mostly just looking out for themselves?
3. Do you think most people would try to take advantage of you if they got a chance, or would they try to be fair?

On the first item, respondents scored 3 for replying "most people can be trusted," 1 for "can't be too careful," and 2 for "don't know" or if not available. On the second, the scoring was 3 for "try to be helpful," 1 for "just look out for themselves," and 2 for "don't know" or if not available. And on the third, 3 for "would try to be fair," 1 for "would take advantage of you," 2 for "don't know" or if not available. Scores on the three items were added to produce a measure on which 9 represented a high level of trust in people and 3 a low level of trust in people.

PERSONAL COMPETENCE

The measure of personal competence was constructed from four items in the NES survey:

1. Do you think it's better to plan your life a good way ahead, or would you say life is too much a matter of luck to plan ahead very far?

2. When you do make plans ahead, do you usually get to carry out things the way you expected, or do things usually come up to make you change your plans?
3. Have you usually felt pretty sure life would work out the way you want it to, or have there been times when you haven't been sure about it?
4. Some people feel they can run their lives pretty much the way they want to; others feel the problems of life are sometimes too big for them. Which ones are you most like?

On the first item, respondents scored 3 for replying "better to plan ahead," 1 for "too much a matter of luck to plan ahead," and 2 for "don't know" or if not available. On the second, the scoring was 3 for "things usually work out as expected," 1 for "have to change plans," and 2 for "don't know" or if not available. On the third, 3 for "felt pretty sure," 1 for "haven't been sure," and 2 for "don't know" or if not available. And on the fourth, 3 for "can run own life," 1 for "problems of life too big," and 2 for "don't know" or if not available. Scores on the four items were added to produce a measure on which 12 represented a strong sense of personal competence and 4 a weak sense of personal competence.

SELF-ESTEEM

The measure of self-esteem was constructed from three items with which respondents were asked to agree or disagree in the BAS survey:

1. On the whole, I am satisfied with myself.
2. At times I think I am no good at all.
3. I sometimes feel that (other) men don't take my opinions seriously.

On the first item, respondents scored 3 for agreement, 1 for disagreement, and 2 for "don't know" or if not available. On the second, the scoring was 3 for disagreement, 1 for agreement, and 2 for "don't know" or if not available. And on the third, 3 for disagreement, 1 for agreement, and 2 for "don't know" or if not available. Scores on the three items were added to produce a measure on which 9 represented a high level of self-esteem and 3 a low level of self-esteem.

TRUST IN GOVERNMENT

The measure of trust in government was constructed from three items in the NES survey:

1. Do you think that people in the government waste a lot of money we pay in taxes, waste some of it, or don't waste very much of it?
2. How much of the time do you think you can trust the government in Washington to do what is right—just about always, most of the time, or only some of the time?
3. Would you say the government is pretty much run by a few big interests looking out for themselves or that it is run for the benefit of all the people?

On the first item, respondents scored 3 for replying "not much"; 1 for "a lot"; and 2 for "some," "don't know," or if not available. On the second, the scoring was 3 for "just about always" or "most of the time;" 1 for "some of the time" or "none of the time;" and 2 for "don't know" or if not available. And on the third, 3 for "for the benefit of all"; 1 for "a few big interests"; and 2 for "don't know," for another response, or if not available. Scores on the three items were added to produce a measure on which 9 represented a high level of trust in government and 3 a low level of trust in government.

POLITICAL TRUST

The measure of political trust was constructed from five pairs of statements in the BAS survey:

1.   *a.* Our government officials usually tell the truth.

    b. Most of the things that government leaders say can't be believed.

2.   *a.* The way our system of government operates, almost every group has a say in running things.

    b. This country is really run by a small number of men at the top who only speak for a few special groups.

3.   *a.* Although our country may be facing difficult times, I still feel that it's a worthwhile place and that I really belong here.

    b. The way this country is going, I often feel that I really don't belong here.

4.   *a.* I am proud of many things about our system of government.

    b. I can't find much in our system of government to be proud of.

5.   *a.* People like me have a fair say in getting the government to do the things we care about.

    b. There is almost no way people like me can have an influence on the government.

Respondents scored 3 for each item on which they chose the first of the pair, 1 for each on which they chose the second of the pair, and 2 for each to which they replied "don't know" or for which a response was not available. Scores on the five items were added to produce a measure on which 15 represented a high level of political trust and 5 a low level of political trust.

EQUALITY AS POLICY

The measure of equality as policy was constructed from two items in the NES survey:

1. How do you feel? Should the government in Washington see to it that black people get fair treatment in jobs or leave these matters to the states and local communities?

2. Do you think the government in Washington should see to it that white and black children go to the same schools or stay out of this area as it is not its business?

On the first item, respondents scored 3 for replying "see to it that black people get fair treatment in jobs" and 1 for "leave these matters to the states and local communities"; respondents who gave other answers were excluded. On the second, the scoring was 3 for "see to it that white and black children go to the same schools" and 1 for "stay out of this area as it is not its business"; respondents who gave other answers were excluded. Scores on the two items were added to produce a measure on which 6 represented a high level of support for equality as policy and 2 a low level of support for equality as policy.

EQUALITY IN PRINCIPLE

The measure of equality in principle was constructed from two items in the NES survey:

1. Which of these statements would you agree with: White people have a right to keep black people out of their neighborhoods if they want to; black people have a right to live wherever they can afford to, just like anybody else.
2. Are you in favor of desegregation, strict segregation, or something in between?

On the first item, respondents scored 3 for replying "black people have a right to live wherever they can afford to," and 1 for "white people have a right to keep black people out"; respondents who gave other answers were excluded. On the second, the scoring was 3 for "desegregation," 2 for "in between," and 1 for "segregation"; respondents who gave other answers were excluded. Scores on the two items were added to produce a measure on which 6 represented a high level of support for equality in principle and 2 a low level of support for equality in principle.

RELIGIOSITY

The measure of religiosity was constructed from two items in the NES survey:

1. Do you believe that God sends misfortune and illness on people as punishment for their sins, or not?
2. Do you feel that someone who doesn't believe in God can be a good American, or not?

On the first item, respondents scored 3 for "yes," 1 for "no," and 2 for "don't know" or if a response was not available. On the second, the scoring was 3 for "no," 1 for "yes," and 2 for "don't know" or if not available. Scores on the two items were added to produce a measure on which 6 represented a high level of religiosity and 2 a low level of religiosity.

EQUALITY OF OPPORTUNITY FOR BLACKS

The measure of equality of opportunity for blacks was constructed from four pairs of statements in the NES survey:

1. *a.* It's lack of skill and abilities that keep many black people from getting a job. It's not just because they're black. When a black person is trained to do something, he is able to get a job.
   b. Many qualified black people can't get a good job. White people with the same skills wouldn't have any trouble.
2. *a.* Many blacks have only themselves to blame for not doing better in life. If they tried harder, they'd do better.
   b. When two qualified people, one black and one white, are considered for the same job, the black won't get the job no matter how hard he tries.
3. *a.* Many black people who don't do well in life do have good training, but the opportunities just always go to whites.
   b. Black people may not have the same opportunities

as whites, but many blacks haven't prepared themselves enough to make use of the opportunities
that come their way.

4.   *a.* Blacks and other minorities no longer face unfair
unemployment conditions. In fact, they are favored in many training and job programs.

     b. Even with the new programs, minorities still face
the same old job discrimination once the program is over.

On the first item, respondents scored 3 for choosing the first
of the pair, 1 for choosing the second of the pair, and 2 for
"don't know" or if a response was not available. On the second
item, the scoring was 3 for the first of the pair, 1 for the second
of the pair, and 2 for "don't know" or if a response was not
available. On the third, 3 for the second of the pair, 1 for the
first of the pair, and 2 for "don't know" or if a response was
not available. On the fourth, 3 for the first of the pair, 1 for
the second of the pair, and 2 for "don't know" or if a response
was not available. Scores on the four items were added to produce a measure on which 12 represented a belief that opportunities for blacks are equal and 2 represented a belief that opportunities for blacks are not equal.

EQUALITY OF OPPORTUNITY FOR WOMEN

The measure of equality of opportunity for women was constructed from three items with which respondents were asked
to agree or disagree in the NES survey:

1. Women have less opportunity than men to get the education for top jobs.
2. Many qualified women can't get good jobs; men with
the same skills have much less trouble.
3. Our society discriminates against women.

Respondents scored 1 for each item with which they agreed a
great deal, 2 for each item with which they agreed somewhat,

4 for each item with which they disagreed somewhat, 5 for each item with which they disagreed a great deal, and 3 for "don't know" or if a response was not available. Scores on the three items were added to produce a measure on which 15 represented a belief that opportunities for women are equal and 3 represented a belief that opportunites for women are not equal.

EQUALITY OF OPPORTUNITY FOR THE POOR

The measure of equality of opportunity for the poor was constructed from three items with which respondents were asked to agree or disagree in the NES survey:

1. With all the training programs and efforts to help the poor, anyone who wants to work can get a job these days.
2. The poor are poor because the American way of life doesn't give all people an equal chance.
3. Poor people didn't have a chance to get a good education — schools in poor neighborhoods are much worse than other schools.

and from two pairs of statements in the NES:

4. *a.* People who are born poor have less chance to get ahead than other people.
   b. People who have the ability and work hard have the same chance as anyone else, even if their parents were poor.
5. *a.* Many poor people simply don't want to work hard.
   b. The poor are poor because the American way of life doesn't give all people an equal chance.

On the first item, respondents scored 3 for agreement, 1 for disagreement, and 2 for "don't know" or if a response was not available. On the second and third, the scoring was 3 for disagreement, 1 for agreement, and 2 for "don't know" or if a response was not available. On the fourth item, respondents scored 3 for "same chance," 1 for "less chance," and 2 for "don't know" or if a response was not available. And on the fifth, the scoring was 3 for "don't want to work hard," 1 for "not an equal chance," and 2 for "don't know" or if a response was not available. Scores on the five items were added to produce a measure on which 15 represented a belief that opportunities for the poor are equal and 3 represented a belief that opportunities for the poor are not equal.

BLACK RESPONSE TO DISCRIMINATION

The measure of black response to discrimination was constructed from two pairs of statements in the NES survey:

1. *a.* Discrimination affects all black people. The only way to handle it is for blacks to organize together and demand rights for all.
   b. Discrimination may affect all blacks but the best way to handle it is for each individual to act like any other American—to work hard, get a good education, and mind his own business.
2. *a.* The best way for blacks to overcome discrimination is through pressure and social action.
   b. The best way to overcome discrimination is for each individual black to be even better trained and more qualified than the most qualified white person.

Respondents scored 3 for each item on which they chose the second of the pair, 1 for each on which they chose the first of the pair, and 2 for each to which they replied "don't know" or for which a response was not available. Scores on the two items were added to produce a measure on which 6 represented a belief that blacks should respond to discrimination individually and 2 represented a belief that blacks should respond to discrimination collectively.

A NOTE ON
ANALYTIC TECHNIQUE

Multiple Classification Analysis (MCA) is the analytic technique that we have chosen. Here we should like to explain why MCA is well suited to answering the kind of question this study asks.

Early in this study, we determined to develop a typology of orientations toward the origins of racial inequality. This is by no means the only tack to take; nor is it always the optimal one. A continuous conception—that is, one concerned with differences of degree rather than of kind—enjoys certain advantages in computational simplicity and power[1]. These advantages notwithstanding, we chose a typological, or discontinuous, approach. Our purposes, quite simply, called for identifying alternative explanations of racial inequality, alternatives that could not themselves be ranked or ordered.

The analysis here focuses on types of explanation as predictors. A typology is, of course, a nominal-level variable; this is the principal reason for our using MCA. MCA is a technique much like regression with dummy variables; however, MCA is expressly designed for analysis of weakly measured (i.e., nominal level) predictors.

In addition, MCA offers an effective way to deal with the problem of correlated predictors. A number of our dependent variables are influenced by type of explanation; however, they are also influenced by other factors—education, for example—which are themselves related to the type of explanation chosen. MCA allows one, first, to see the relation between predictor

145

and outcome, then to see the adjusted scores when the covariate is statistically removed.

For a comprehensive discussion of MCA, the reader should consult Frank M. Andrews, James N. Morgan, John Sonquist, and Laura Klem, *Multiple Classification Analysis: A Report on a Computer Program for Multiple Regression Using Categorical Predictors* (Ann Arbor, Mich.: Institute for Social Research, 1973).

NOTE

1. For an excellent example of the benefits of such an approach applied to a similar problem, see Stanley Feldman, "Economic Individualism and Mass Belief Systems" (paper prepared for delivery at the Annual Meeting of the Midwest Political Science Association, Cincinnati, Ohio, 14-18 April 1981).

BIBLIOGRAPHY

ACHEN, CHRISTOPHER H. "Mass Attitudes and the Survey Response." *American Political Science Review* 69 (1975): 1218-31.

ADORNO, T.W.; ELSE FRENKEL-BRUNSWIK; DANIEL J. LEVINSON; and R. NEVITT SANFORD. *The Authoritarian Personality.* New York: Norton, 1950.

ANDREWS, FRANK M.; JAMES N. MORGAN; JOHN SONQUIST; and LAURA KLEM. *Multiple Classification Analysis: A Report on a Computer Program for Multiple Regression Using Categorical Predictors.* Ann Arbor, Mich.: Institute for Social Research, 1973.

APOSTLE, RICHARD A.; CHARLES Y. GLOCK; THOMAS PIAZZA; and MARIJEAN SUELZLE. *The Anatomy of Racial Attitudes.* Berkeley: University of California Press, 1983.

ARIELI, YEHOSHUA. *Individualism and Nationalism in American Ideology.* Baltimore: Penguin, 1964.

BENNETT, W. LANCE. *Public Opinion in American Politics.* New York: Harcourt Brace Jovanovich, 1980.

BERCOVITCH, SACVAN. *The American Jeremiad.* Madison: University of Wisconsin Press, 1978.

BISHOP, GEORGE F.; ALFRED J. TUCHFARBER; and ROBERT W. OLDENDICK. "Change in the Structure of American Political Attitudes: The Nagging Question of Question Wording." *American Journal of Political Science* 22 (1978): 250-69.

_____; and STEPHEN E. BENNETT. "Questions about Question Wording." *American Journal of Political Science* 23 (1979): 187-92.

BRODY, RICHARD A., and PAUL M. SNIDERMAN. "From Life Space to Polling Place: The Relevance of Personal Concerns for Voting Behavior." *British Journal of Political Science* 7 (1977): 337-60.

BROWN, PETER. *The Cult of the Saints.* Chicago: University of Chicago Press, 1981.

BURSTEIN, PAUL. "Public Opinion, Demonstrations, and the Passage of Antidiscrimination Legislation." *Public Opinion Quarterly* 43 (1979): 157-72.

CAMPBELL, ANGUS; PHILIP E. CONVERSE; WARREN E. MILLER; and DONALD E. STOKES. *The American Voter.* New York: Wiley, 1960.

CARMINES, EDWARD G., and JAMES A. STIMSON. "Racial Issues and the Structure of Mass Belief Systems." *Journal of Politics* 44 (1982): 2-20.

CHONG, DENNIS; HERBERT MCCLOSKY; and JOHN ZALLER. "Patterns of Support for Democratic and Capitalist Values in the United States." *British Journal of Political Science* 13 (1983): 402-40.

CITRIN, JACK; HERBERT MCCLOSKY; J. MERRILL SHANKS; and PAUL M. SNIDERMAN. "Personal and Political Sources of Political Alienation." *British Journal of Political Science* 5 (1975): 1-31.

CONVERSE, PHILIP E. "The Nature of Belief Systems in Mass Publics." In *Ideology and Discontent,* ed. David E. Apter. New York: Free Press, 1964.

CROWELL, JOHN, and STANFORD J. SEARLE, eds. *The Responsibility of Mind in a Civilization of Machines: Essays by Perry Miller.* Amherst: University of Massachusetts Press, 1979.

DAVIES, A.F. *Skills, Outlooks and Passions.* Cambridge, England: Cambridge University Press, 1980.

ERIKSON, ROBERT S.; NORMAN R. LUTTBEG; and KENT TEDIN. *American Public Opinion.* 2d ed. New York: Wiley, 1980.

FEHRENBACHER, DON E., ed. *History and American Society: Essays of David M. Potter.* New York: Oxford University Press, 1973.

FELDMAN, STANLEY. "Economic Individualism and Mass Belief

Systems." Paper prepared for delivery at the Annual Meeting of the Midwest Political Science Association, Cincinnati, Ohio, 15-18 April 1981.

———. "Economic Self-Interest and Political Behavior." *American Journal of Political Science* 26 (1982): 446-66.

FIELD, JOHN O., and RONALD E. ANDERSON. "Ideology in the Public's Conception of the 1964 Election." *Public Opinion Quarterly* 33 (1969): 380-98.

FIORINA, MORRIS P. *Retrospective Voting in American National Elections.* New Haven: Yale University Press, 1981.

GLOCK, CHARLES Y., and RODNEY STARK. *Christian Beliefs and Anti-Semitism.* New York: Harper & Row, 1966.

HANSEN, JOHN J. "The Fundamentalist Personality." Honors thesis, Department of Political Science, Stanford University, 1981.

HOCHSCHILD, JENNIFER. *What's Fair?* Cambridge, Mass.: Harvard University Press, 1981.

HOFSTADTER, RICHARD. *Anti-Intellectualism in American Life.* New York: Vintage Books, 1962.

———. *Social Darwinism in American Thought.* Boston: Beacon Press, 1955.

———. *The Paranoid Style in American Politics.* New York: Vintage Books, 1967.

HUNTINGTON, SAMUEL P. *American Politics: The Promise of Disharmony.* Cambridge, Mass.: Belknap Press, 1981.

HYMAN, HERBERT H., and CHARLES R. WRIGHT. *Education's Lasting Influence on Values.* Chicago: University of Chicago Press, 1979.

INGLEHART, RONALD. *The Silent Revolution.* Princeton: Princeton University Press, 1977.

INKELES, ALEX. "Continuity and Change in American National Character." In *The Third Century: America as a Post-Industrial Society,* ed. Seymour Martin Lipset. Chicago: University of Chicago Press, 1979.

JACKMAN, MARY R. "Education and Policy Commitment to Racial Integration." *American Journal of Political Science* 25 (1981): 256-69.

———. "General and Applied Tolerance: Does Education Increase Commitment to Racial Integration?" *American Journal of Political Science* 22 (1978): 302-24.

LANE, ROBERT E. "Patterns of Political Belief." In *Handbook of Political Psychology*, ed. Jeanne N. Knutson. San Francisco: Jossey-Bass, 1973.

―――, and DAVID O. SEARS. *Public Opinion*. Englewood Cliffs, N.J.: Prentice-Hall, 1964.

LEWIS, MICHAEL. *The Culture of Inequality*. Amherst: University of Massachusetts Press, 1978.

LIPSET, SEYMOUR MARTIN. *The First New Nation: The United States in Historical and Comparative Perspective*. New York: Norton, 1979.

―――. "The Wavering Polls." In *Public Opinion and Public Policy*, ed. Norman R. Luttbeg. Itasca, Ill.: Peacock, 1981. Pp. 353-67.

McCLOSKY, HERBERT. "Consensus and Ideology in American Politics." *American Political Science Review* 58 (1964): 361-82.

―――. "Conservatism and Personality." *American Political Science Review* 52 (1958): 27-45.

―――, and CHARLES A. BANN. "On the Reappraisal of the Classical Conservatism Scale." *Political Methodology* 6 (1979): 149-72.

―――, and ALIDA BRILL. *Dimensions of Tolerance*. New York: Russell Sage Foundation, 1983.

―――, and JOHN ZALLER. *The American Ethos: Public Attitudes toward Capitalism and Democracy*. Cambridge, Mass.: Harvard University Press, 1984.

―――; PAUL J. HOFFMAN; and ROSEMARY O'HARA. "Issue Conflict and Consensus among Party Leaders and Followers." *American Political Science Review* 54 (1960): 406-27.

McCONAHAY, JOHN B. "Self-Interest versus Racial Attitudes as Correlates of Anti-Busing Attitudes in Louisville: Is It the Buses or the Blacks? "*Journal of Politics* 44 (1982): 692-720.

MARSDEN, GEORGE M. *Fundamentalism and American Culture*. New York: Oxford University Press, 1980.

MILLER, PERRY. *Errand into the Wilderness*. Cambridge, Mass.: Harvard University Press, 1956.

_____. *The American Transcendentalists.* Garden City, N.Y.: Anchor Books, 1957.

MILLER, WARREN E., and TERESA E. LEVITIN. *Leadership and Change: The New Politics and the American Electorate.* Cambridge, Mass.: Winthrop, 1976.

MILLER, WARREN E.; ARTHUR H. MILLER; and EDWARD J. SCHNEIDER. *American National Election Studies Data Sourcebook.* Cambridge, Mass.: Harvard University Press, 1980.

MYRDAL, GUNNAR. *An American Dilemma: The Negro Problem and Modern Democracy.* New York: Harper & Bros., 1944.

NIE, NORMAN H., and KRISTI ANDERSEN. "Mass Belief Systems Revisited: Political Change and Attitude Structure." *Journal of Politics* 36 (1974): 540-90.

NIE, NORMAN H.; SIDNEY VERBA; and JOHN R. PETROCIK. *The Changing American Voter.* Cambridge, Mass.: Harvard University Press, 1976.

PAGE, BENJAMIN I. *Choices and Echoes in Presidential Elections.* Chicago: University of Chicago Press, 1978.

_____, and RICHARD A. BRODY. "Policy Voting and the Electoral Process: The Vietnam War Issue." *American Political Science Review* 66 (1972): 979-95.

PIERCE, JOHN C., and PAUL R. HAGNER. "Conceptualization and Party Identification: 1956-1976." *American Journal of Political Science* 26 (1982): 377-87.

PIERSON, GEORGE WILSON. *Tocqueville in America.* Gloucester, Mass.: Peter Smith, 1969.

ROKEACH, MILTON. *Belief, Attitudes and Values.* San Francisco: Jossey-Bass, 1968.

_____. *The Nature of Human Values.* New York: Free Press, 1973.

ROSENBERG, MORRIS. *The Logic of Survey Analysis.* New York: Basic Books, 1968.

SCHLOZMAN, KAY LEHMAN, and SIDNEY VERBA. *Injury to Insult.* Cambridge, Mass.: Harvard University Press, 1979.

SCHUMAN, HOWARD, and STANLEY PRESSER. *Questions and Answers in Attitude Surveys.* New York: Academic Press, 1981.

SEARS, DAVID O., and DONALD R. KINDER. "Racial Tensions and Voting in Los Angeles." In *Los Angeles: Viability and Prospects for Metropolitan Leadership*, ed. Werner Hirsch. New York: Praeger, 1971.

SEARS, DAVID O., and JACK CITRIN. *Tax Revolt.* Cambridge, Mass.: Harvard University Press, 1982.

SEARS, DAVID O.; CARL P. HENSLER; and LESLIE K. SPEER. "Whites' Opposition to 'Busing': Self-Interest or Symbolic Politics?" *American Political Science Review* 73 (1979): 369-84.

SEARS, DAVID O.; RICHARD R. LAU; TOM R. TYLER; and HARRIS M. ALLEN, JR. "Self-Interest vs. Symbolic Politics in Policy Attitudes and Presidential Voting." *American Political Science Review* 74 (1980): 670-84.

SELZNICK, GERTRUDE J., and STEPHEN STEINBERG. *The Tenacity of Prejudice.* New York: Harper & Row, 1969.

SHILS, EDWARD. "The Antinomies of Liberalism." In *The Relevance of Liberalism,* ed. Research Institute on International Change. Boulder, Colo.: Westview Press, 1978.

SMITH, ERIC R.A.N. "The Levels of Conceptualization: False Measures of Ideological Sophistication." *American Political Science Review* 74 (1980): 685-96.

SNIDERMAN, PAUL M. *A Question of Loyalty.* Berkeley: University of California Press, 1982.

————. *Personality and Democratic Politics.* Berkeley: University of California Press, 1975.

————, and RICHARD A. BRODY. "Coping: The Ethic of Self-Reliance." *American Journal of Political Science* 21 (1977): 501-21.

————; RICHARD A. BRODY; and JAMES H. KUKLINSKI. "Policy Reasoning and Political Values: Problem of Racial Equality." *American Journal of Political Science* (1984): 75-94.

————, and PHILIP E. TETLOCK. "Symbolic Racism: Problems of Political Motive Attribution." *Journal of Social Issues,* in press.

STIMSON, JAMES A. "Belief Systems: Constraint, Complexity, and the 1972 Election." *American Journal of Political Science* 19 (1975): 383-418.

SULLIVAN, JOHN L.; JAMES E. PIERESON; and GEORGE E. MAR-
CUS. "Ideological Constraint in the Mass Public: A Methodological Critique and Some New Findings." *American
Journal of Political Science* 22 (1978): 233-49.
_____; and STANLEY FELDMAN. "The More Things Change,
the More They Stay the Same: The Stability of Mass Be-
lief Systems." *American Journal of Political Science* 23
(1979): 176-86.
WEINER, BERNARD. "A Cognitive (Attribution)—Emotion—
Action Model of Motivated Behavior: An Analysis of Judg-
ments of Help-Giving." *Journal of Personality and Social
Psychology* 29 (1980): 186-200.
WESTIN, ALAN F. "The John Birch Society." In *The Radical
Right,* ed. Daniel Bell. Garden City, N.Y.: Anchor Books,
1964, 239-68.
WILSON, GLENN D., ed. *The Psychology of Conservatism.* New
York: Academic Press, 1973.
WOLFINGER, RAYMOND E., and STEVEN J. ROSENSTONE. *Who
Votes?* New Haven: Yale University Press, 1980.
WOLFINGER, RAYMOND E.; MARTIN SHAPIRO; and FRED I.
GREENSTEIN. *Dynamics of American Politics.* 2d ed. Engle-
wood Cliffs, N.J.: Prentice-Hall, 1980.

INDEX

Speer, Leslie K., 118, 152
Spencer, Herbert, 99
Stark, Rodney, 103, 149
Steinberg, Stephen, 113, 118, 152
Stimson, James A., 13, 25, 148, 152
Stokes, Donald E., 23, 148
Suelzle, Marijean, 23, 147
Sullivan, John L., 23, 24, 153
Sumner, William Graham, 99-100
Symbolic racism. *See* Racism

Tedin, Kent L., 9, 23, 148
Tetlock, Philip E., 118, 152
Thoreau, Henry David, 100-101
Tocqueville, Alexis de, 3, 34, 35, 99
Traditionalism, 54-55, 107-8
Transcendentalism, 100

Trust in government. *See* Government, attitudes toward
Trust in people, 65-67, 68, 108, 133
Tuchfarber, Alfred J., 24, 147
Turner, Frederick Jackson, 99
Tyler, Tom R., 118, 152

Verba, Sidney, 23, 26, 58, 151
Voluntarism, 109-10, 117

Weiner, Bernard, 102, 118, 153
Westin, Alan F., 78, 153
Wilson, Glenn D., 77, 153
Wolfinger, Raymond E., 7, 127, 128, 153
Wright, Charles R., 102, 149

Zaller, John, 25, 148, 150

ABOUT THE AUTHORS

MICHAEL GRAY HAGEN grew up in Eau Claire, Wisconsin. He received his B.A. in political science from Stanford University in 1981 and is now a Ph.D. candidate in the Department of Political Science at the University of California, Berkeley.

PAUL M. SNIDERMAN is a professor of political science at Stanford University. He received his B.A. in philosophy from the University of Toronto and his Ph.D. in political science from the University of California, Berkeley. He has been a Guggenheim Fellow and a Fellow of the Center for Advanced Studies in the Behavioral Sciences.